A Year of

Free Love

Living the dream of racehorse ownership
on a shoestring budget
By Tony Linnett

Joseph Linnett, the author's youngest son, with Free Love

For my dear wife, Jennie, and my three children Matthew, Celia and Joseph, who have not only tolerated my passion but joined in the fun as well. And for Sea Pigeon, who lit the flame more than forty years ago.

Published by Tony Linnett 2019

Printed by Catford Print Centre
3 Bellingham Road
Catford
London
SE6 2PN

ISBN 978-1-5272-4027-8

A Year of Free Love

Contents

1 The Plan

2 September 2017

I was lost. Not very lost, but I was in Old Station Road, Newmarket, and according to Google Maps I should have been right on top of Tom's stables. Pete couldn't make sense of it either. You would have thought the entrance to a racing yard would have been obvious but all I could see were terraced houses punctuated by the occasional shop. Beyond the white façade of a large and impressive Georgian building on the left (surely not Tom's?), the road bore right, turning away from a quiet and empty heath. After a slow drive back towards town, I reluctantly threw in the towel and decided to ask for help.

Old Station Road was hardly bustling, and I couldn't find a passer-by to quiz. Maybe the Newmarket inhabitants were hiding somewhere with their horses, and it seemed more sensible to try Tom's mobile. He quickly pointed us in the right direction assuring me that it was an easy mistake to make. The stable entrance was at the end of Moulton Road, not on Old Station Road at all. After turning right at the imposing Queen Victoria Golden Jubilee clocktower which overlooks the roundabout at the top of the high street, I must have whizzed past the left fork which led to the bottom of Newmarket's famous gallops. We turned around and were soon parked up at the back of a whitewashed brick building which I assumed was Tom's yard.

I had already been in touch with Tom about our plan in an email at the end of last month:

Hi Tom,

A small group of friends (five or six of us) would like to buy a yearling in October. Before you get too excited, we think our budget is around the 10,000 guineas mark which puts us very much in Tattersalls Book 3 territory. We can't afford a slow-burner so would be looking for a speedy pedigree and the possibility of the horse being able to run from May/June onwards, health and good fortune permitting.

Is this something you could help us with? Some of us have been involved in syndicates before but we like the idea of doing the whole thing from scratch. We would need help buying the yearling at the sales. Do you do this yourself or use agents and what additional costs would there be at the point of purchase?
Regards, Tony

Tom's reply had been prompt, and encouraging:
Hello Tony,
Thanks for getting in touch, this sounds great and is a similar type that Jackie and I have already bought and like to buy. As you say, Book 3 is a good option, a good advantage of it is the £150K race at Newmarket in October, which is nice to target. There is a sale at Ascot on 12 September as well that includes the Book 3 race.

Jackie and I go to all the sales looking for value and we buy some ourselves and sometimes we use an agent. It's really up to the owners what they prefer. Agents charge a 5% fee of the cost of the horse for their services. We are free. If you have time and want to meet up, let's see if we can put a date in the diary.
Best regards, Tom

I arranged to make a preliminary visit to Tom's yard and report back to the others in our fledgling partnership. Luckily, Pete was able to keep me company. For me and Pete, Newmarket and back could be done in a morning from Dartford. It would be a flying visit and we didn't expect to be with Tom for more than half an hour for what was essentially a fact-finding mission. We wouldn't be signing on the dotted line today, but the fact that Tom understood our circumstances and budgetary restrictions was promising, as was his willingness to meet up in person to talk things through.

As we entered the yard, Tom walked out to greet us. He looked leaner than his photograph on the Tom Clover Racing website. Perhaps that's what the stress of training racehorses does to you. I thought he was probably in his late twenties, but with his mop of dark hair and boyish looks, he might easily be asked for ID at the door of a local nightclub.

I suggested Tom to the other boys because he had made a promising start in his first season going it alone, following a six-year stint as assistant trainer to the highly successful Newmarket handler, David Simcock. I had also picked up from his website that his partner was Jackie Jarvis, the daughter of the late Michael Jarvis who had trained Carrol House to win the 1989 Arc de Triomphe. I'm pretty sure Jackie wasn't born when dad's chestnut superstar triumphed in Paris, but I bet she grew up in a house full of photos, trophies and equine memorabilia which gave her a vicarious share in her father's great day. She had also done some work for her dad's successor, the increasingly successful Roger Varian. Tom Clover and Jackie Jarvis was a partnership steeped in racing.

Tom greeted us warmly and welcomed us to his rented base, the historic Wroughton House Stables which, now long-forgotten, was responsible for a nineteenth century Derby winner in George Frederick. The yard has 25 boxes and its location is enviable, situated a pitching iron away from the famous Warren Hill gallop. He and Jackie seemed to be well-established there. All the boxes were full, and Tom gave us a little tour, dwelling at some of them to tell us a bit about their inmates and what they had achieved. There was Hunni, a two-year-old filly who had won a valuable nursery handicap for a group similar to ours. There were high hopes that some of the older handicappers could win again and we paused to give a pat or two to Music Maestro and the recently acquired Balgair. Tom knew them all well and his interest in them as individuals was sincere. Here was a young trainer who was quietly passionate and naturally hands-on. The vibes felt good.

Back in the office, Jackie offered coffee which she made with a smart looking machine, apparently a present from an affluent, coffee-loving owner. It sat incongruously in the cramped, busy office with its muddy carpet and piles of racing paraphernalia. Pete later remarked, rather unkindly, that a hoover might have been a more appropriate gift.

We went through our plan with Tom and Jackie over tea and coffee but there wasn't a great deal more to be discussed at this stage. We needed to give our feedback to the others before deciding to go ahead. If that was the case, we agreed that it would be a good idea for all the owners to make a visit to Tom's just before next month's yearling sales. Everyone could bring their questions to that gathering.

Tom had a question of his own before we left. He was curious why a group of owners, based in different parts of the country, had decided to approach him about buying a horse. There had been no personal recommendation as far as he could see. I explained that we were aiming to take a chance with an up and coming trainer whose fees were likely to be competitive and who was willing to give us some time. I'd also noted the promising start he had made last season, particularly with a couple of two-year-olds. It was a measured punt, in other words.

3 September 2017

By now we had established that there would be five of us. A possible sixth member of the partnership, Derek Maidment, had decided against it, preferring to concentrate on the share he already had in Itoldyou, a staying steeplechaser trained by Linda Jewell in the bucolic Kentish setting of Sutton Valence. That had an obvious impact on our budget as I explained in a detailed email I sent to the others:

Gents,

Here's an update following the visit Pete and I made to Tom Clover's yard in Newmarket on Saturday morning. I can't possibly cover everything discussed in this email but will try my best to give a synopsis of the story to date.

First of all, Tom came across well as a young and ambitious trainer who is realistic about what he can achieve during this early stage of his career. He was very open to our limited budget plan and fully understood the need for us to purchase a yearling at the October sales that will have the potential to be an early two-year-old. We are therefore looking at pedigrees with speed rather than stamina.

It might be best if I try to continue by listing the key proposals to date.

1. There are currently 5 of us in the partnership and the proposal is that we all contribute £6,000 to the project. The partners are: Tony Linnett, Peter Smith, Trevor Wyatt, Patrick Hickey and Mick Corringham.

2. We need to set a purchase price for the yearling and I think that we should be aiming at no more than 10,000 guineas, which is around the median price of Book 3 yearlings.

3. It's proposed that we buy a filly as they are cheaper and may have a residual value for potential breeders should we need to sell the horse on at the end of next season. The partnership will be for a year initially.

4. Tom will bid on our behalf at the sale but we are welcome to attend and give some recommendations in advance regarding anything that we might be interested in. If you have a look at the Tattersalls website, you can access the electronic catalogue for Book 3 and look up the pedigrees of all the yearlings for sale.

5 Everyone would need to contribute at least £3,000 in the first instance to cover the purchase of the filly and the first few months training. We can then set dates for further contributions.

6 We need to set up an account from which we can pay Tom's bills and we can also make our top-up contributions to the agreed figure of £6,000. I will probably put the whole lot in at the beginning, but I guess it is up to individuals what they want to do

7. Tom's fees are as follows: £50 a day plus £120 a month for access to the gallops and about £80 a month for shoes. That puts the monthly figure at around £1,750 (before VAT) but if and when the filly is ready to race there will be entry, transport and jockey fees to meet.

8. I reckon £23-24k for a whole season is a fair estimate which would mean a top up in the final month or two if we went to 10,000 guineas for the purchase. That's all assuming that the filly wins no prize money whatsoever, and we really have to work on that basis. She may end up being very moderate and going to the sales in October leaving us all £6k out of pocket but richer for the experience!

I think we have a real goer here. It would be preferable if we could meet up at the stables before the sales (October 12-14) to talk about things. In the meantime, have a look at Tom Clover's website and the one for Tattersalls where you can browse through the pedigrees of sales entries for hours and hours and hours. Have fun!

Regards, Tony

6 October 2017

We somehow managed to find a day when all five of us could get to Newmarket to meet up with Tom and Jackie and discuss every aspect of our project. Despite considering other partners, in the end it was just the five of us who formed the syndicate. With an eye on spreading the financial load, we could have looked for one or two more, but all agreed that the larger the group, the more diluted the experience. Although I had enjoyed my previous involvement with racing clubs, this was going to be very different.

One of the gang of five was an old school friend. Patrick and I have very fond memories of using some of our sixth-form study lessons to amble back to one of our homes to watch the televised racing. In those days it was just the big meetings that were covered and only by ITV or BBC, of course. Patrick's dad, Joe, owned a free off licence in Sidcup which closed in the afternoon ahead of the evening trade and he was often about when we watched the racing. Joe loved a bet and took a keen interest in the racing presented by John Rickman, John (Lord) Oaksey, Brough Scott, Julian Wilson, Peter O'Sullivan and other broadcasting legends of the past. If it was at my house, my dear departed mum made us tea and biscuits and asked us chatty questions about school while we stared intently at the grainy pictures transmitted from Cheltenham, Ascot or Newmarket. What great memories. Comedy Of Errors regaining the Champion Hurdle in 1975. Roman Warrior carrying top-weight to victory in the Ayr Gold Cup that same year. I can remember those heroic triumphs more clearly than Charlton Athletic's home game against AFC Wimbledon last season. That might be an age thing, though. Or a Charlton thing.

My mum took no notice of the racing but took great interest in her three boys and their friends. In fact, she took great interest in everyone, so it was no great surprise that her funeral at St Lawrence's church, Sidcup in February 2016 took place before a packed congregation. Everyone knew and loved Monica Linnett.

In his early twenties Patrick was relocated to Leeds with the Civil Service and, a little later, bought a house in York with his lifetime partner, Sally. Needless to say, a few of us have been descending ever since on the happy couple, normally in August for the big Ebor meeting. Patrick's interest in racing endured beyond school and he was a natural to be involved with our ownership project. Like me and Pete, he had dabbled with small-scale ownership through racing clubs, but he too was keen to be involved at a more personal level. If you are with a racing club, there may be up to 30 of you in the parade ring trying to catch what the trainer or jockey are saying. You don't really have much say in future races as that is all left to the manager of the club. What we wanted was the full involvement that a small ownership group could provide.

The meeting with Tom and Jackie took place just six days before the start of the Tattersalls Book 3 sales. We aimed for an 11am rendezvous and were more or less on time. Patrick and Mick drove down from York while me, Pete and Trevor shared a car from Dartford. Our northern partners definitely had the short straw with their three-hour journey, but I think Patrick and Mick thought it was worth every minute. We had a good look around the yard, borrowing a horse to pose with for a group photo. Afterwards, we had a helpful chat about some of the admin that needed to be done. Jackie's racing office experience was invaluable here.

The sale sounded as if it be should straightforward enough. Tom and Jackie would bid on our behalf and I would need to register our ownership with the BHA once we had made a purchase. There was all the other stuff about banking, insurance, and claiming back VAT that needed to be sorted out as well.

We went through everything. Pete's somewhat cautious and fastidious nature prompted him to enquire about insurance, contracts and all aspects of financial management. I was too excited to dwell for very long on these matters. All I wanted was a horse.

After our visit, the five of us ended up in the Old Wellington pub, a neat and friendly local at the end of Old Station Road. Over a pint and a sandwich, we agreed to go with Tom and use his help to buy a yearling at next week's yearling sales. I'm not sure what we would have done if our visit had thrown up reservations about proceeding. There wasn't a plan B at this stage. We were taking a chance with a young trainer but with only 25 horses in his care, we felt confident that we would receive a more personal touch, and his stabling fees would be reasonably competitive when compared with some of the Newmarket heavyweights. In any event, I'm sure Sir Michael Stoute wouldn't be greatly enthused by our budget or desire to buy a speedy early season type. That's not really his style.

Trevor, Pete, Tony, Mick and Patrick pose with an inmate during the visit to Tom Clover's Wroughton House stables in Newmarket.

11 October 2017

Tomorrow was the big day. I'd be up early and off to Newmarket for the Tattersalls Book 3 Yearling Sales where the adventure would begin. But I suppose it really started with Sea Pigeon's first novice hurdle win in 1974, or Wollow's demolition of the Dewhurst Stakes field at Newmarket in the autumn of 1975 when I was a wide-eyed seventeen-year-old. Or perhaps it was on a sunny day at Folkestone racecourse in 2007 when I was introduced to Heart of the South Racing and penny-share ownership. It's hard to be precise. I just knew that the dream of racehorse ownership would come to fruition on Thursday 12 October 2017.

For those with an interest in horse racing, I'm sure Tattersalls, the leading bloodstock auctioneers in Europe, need no introduction. Based in Newmarket where the racehorse population runs into thousands and many jobs are entirely dependent on the breeding and training of thoroughbred racehorses, their October yearling sales attract regally-bred young horses and owners with deep pockets. The amounts of money people are prepared to exchange for a young horse which may, on maturity, be able to run a bit faster than its four-legged contemporaries, defies reason.

I noted that the top price at the Book 1 sale, held four days ago, was four million guineas for a filly by Galileo out of Sir Michael's globetrotting superstar, Dank. The final cost to the new owner (no prizes for guessing it was Godolphin) was therefore £4,200,000 once the auctioneer's handy 5% commission had been paid. Both mum and dad were prolifically successful at the highest level but, as far as I can see, over a year later their young daughter has yet to set foot on a racecourse. Another expensive purchase was a son of Dubawi, a colt out of the Arc de Triomphe winner Danedream. He cost one and a half million guineas and made his belated racecourse appearance a year later finishing sixth of 12 beaten more than 10 lengths in a modest Newmarket novice race. The Racing Post analyst suggested that his speculative Epsom Derby entry didn't seem very realistic at the moment. But he could improve. We all travel in hope.

It's not a surprise that many people are bewildered by the huge prices paid for babies in the hope that they may turn out to be future champions, or even the more modest amounts paid by those with the same expansive dreams, but with limited funds and access therefore restricted to young horses with less regal breeding. Of course, people get lucky every once in a while. Mrs Danvers was bought for just 1,000 guineas as a yearling in 2015 and went on to win around £200,000 in prize money, capturing Newbury's Super Sprint and the Group 3 Cornwallis Stakes at Newmarket during her short but fabulous career.

At the other end of the scale, the casualty rates are attritional. Who can forget Snaffi Dancer? A son of the legendary sire Northern Dancer, this young colt cost Sheik Mohammed $10.2 million at Kentucky's Keenland sales in 1983. When the Sheik's expensive potential superstar went into training, it soon became apparent that he was too slow to catch a cold and entering him in races wasn't even considered. Apparently, he was given a chance at stud but sired just four foals after suffering from fertility problems. It can happen whether you have ten thousand or ten million to spend.

There are good financial reasons why many wouldn't give ownership a second thought, but being involved in some way still appeals to plenty and has its roots in a rich history, unique to our part of the world. Even in an age when most of us have little or no contact with horses, it's clear that racing still fires the imagination of young and old, rich and poor. In a country where football is king, horseracing remains the second biggest spectator sport and you only have to go to the Cheltenham Festival in March, or York in August, to feel the intensity of interest, the adrenalin-fuelled engagement of the crowd, the adoration of true equine greats and the admiration for the men and women who ride them.

Of course, the sport means different things to different people. Some have a genuine love of horses and have grown up with them. Others enjoy the challenge of studying form. After all, picking a winner and having a bet is an integral part of the racing experience. Let's not be coy, most people who go racing or who follow it on the television, bet on horses. There's nothing wrong with that. I'm a regular punter myself, but to small stakes and never bet more than I can afford to lose. Last, but not least, is the casual racegoer whose occasional visit to leafy Lingfield or breezy Brighton is no more than a fun day out. They're the ones that racing needs to hold on to.

For me, racing is a lot of these things, but I suppose I've been swept up by the romance of the sport as well. I fell in love with the thoroughbred racehorse a long time ago. I don't ride, I don't look after horses, I haven't got a connection with the countryside, having lived all my life in provincial towns or suburbia. But when I lean on the paddock rail at Sandown Park and watch those elegant creatures in the parade ring before they race against each other at breath-taking speeds, I know I am witnessing something very special. I am part of a living history in which every horse's pedigree and performance are meticulously recorded. Their family trees are laden with the heroes and heroines of the past. Nearly all of them trace back to just three stallions imported into England from the Middle East in the late 17th and early 18th centuries: the Byerley Turk, the Darley Arabian, and the Godolphin Arabian. Nearly all of them. Even the one we were going to buy tomorrow.

2 Lot 1383

12 October 2017

It was just me and Pete who were able to get to Newmarket for the first day of the Tattersalls Book 3 sales. Trevor and Patrick were tied up with work, and Mick was unable to make the journey down from York, so it was up to the pair of us to make sure that we didn't return empty handed.

Pete is an old University of Reading friend who lives around the corner from me in Dartford, a town with a rich history and plenty of good features, but it was the tunnel and bridge that really put the place on the modern map, and not in a good way either. Pete was on the same history and politics course as me and I discovered soon enough that we had a common interest in racing. 'Do you fancy anything for the Hennessy?' seemed a much more interesting ice-breaker than, 'And how are you getting on with your Hegel and Marx essay?' We had quite a few outings to racecourses while at Reading, including going to Newbury during our first term to see Zeta's Son land the 1976 Hennessy Gold Cup.

Pete's a west country boy whose family home was near Chippenham. His dad, the late and larger than life John Smith, enjoyed his racing and I remember being taken by him and Pete's mum, Margaret, to the Beaufort point to point meeting one bitterly cold March. I made John's day when I stared rather queasily at what appeared to be birds' feet protruding from the pastry of a so-called rook pie, a helping of which I declined. God knows what was in it, but it was just the sort of thing to make a townie feel out of their comfort zone and I think John revelled in my suburban unease.

Margaret's still going strong, remaining physically and mentally agile, and we often see her at Christmas as for a number of years the

Linnett and Smith families have hosted festivities on an alternating basis. I think 17 was the biggest gathering - at the Smiths, thank God. We've been on holiday many times with Pete and Melanie and their two boys who remain good friends with our three children. They are some of our longest known and closest friends, so it was inevitable that the aspiration for racehorse ownership would involve Pete.

I say that, but Pete's caution with money and risk-averse nature aren't features usually associated with racehorse owners. I vividly remember persuading him that Be My Guest had a sure-fire look about him in the 1977 Derby trial at Epsom in April. We both backed the horse, each having a pound on the nose. I suppose that's the equivalent of around £10 today as I reckon one of those lovely old green pound notes would buy you three or four pints of bitter in the student union bar. Anyway, Lester Piggott steered Be My Guest to a comfortable victory at 9/4 and we went to the local bookies to collect our £3.25 winnings. As we picked up, I was already calculating how many pints I had just won and was about to discuss with Pete where we should celebrate. But he'd vanished. It was quite a while before he reappeared clutching his building society savings book. He had deposited £2 into his account with the remaining 25p profit retained in cash. Clearly Pete would be able to buy himself a celebratory pint out of his winnings, but I would have to fend for myself.

I suppose it's fair to describe Pete as the careful one. You may ask what prompted him to stump up an initial £6K for our horse project, but he's always shown interest in a plan that's been in the pipeline for years. Being made redundant from his Health Service job just months before he was going to retire anyway, provided him with a windfall he'd given up hope of catching. It was important that I got him to sign up before he had a change of heart, deciding that a new roof or driveway would be a better, if slightly more mundane, investment.

The roads were clear - even the infamous Dartford crossing behaved itself - and we approached Newmarket in plenty of time for the sales which started at 9.30am. Everything about Newmarket leaves you in no doubt that this is the home of British horse racing. Travellers coming to the town from the south are greeted by an enormous horse and groom statue in the middle of a vast roundabout where a left turn takes you to the July Course and the National Stud. It's straight on for the town and the many training yards which cluster around the famous gallops cut into the heath.

This was all new territory for me. I'd never been to a bloodstock sale before, but I had some idea of what to expect having spent hours and hours researching the pedigrees of the yearlings for sale. They all had lot numbers and stables allocated to them. In theory, we could turn up and ask for one of the yearlings to be taken out of its box and walked in front of us so that we could have a good look at what we might be bidding for. In practice, this would have been a complete waste of time as neither of us would have a clue what to look for. I guess we might have spotted if a leg was missing but years of going racing has helped me develop only a very rudimentary knowledge of what to look for when watching horses in the parade ring before they run.

We found the Tattersalls complex easily enough. It's tucked away behind Newmarket High Street but occupies a large mound of land, with its distinctive, hexagonal shaped sales building perched on the summit. I drove cautiously into the car park, not quite sure where to go or even if we were entitled to be there. I was relieved that my 2014 Vauxhall Zafira didn't look too out of place, which was an a ridiculously insecure thought. But should I have a badge, a pass or something that proved I was a bona fide visitor?

We stepped out into the sunlight. It was a glorious morning; one of those days that makes you grateful for the absurdly unpredictable climate we have in our little corner of the planet. We could see the sales ring at the top of the hill, an iconic building resembling a postwar catholic church or similar place of worship. That's where we were heading, but I half expected to be stopped by one of the yellow hi-vis clad stewards and asked if I needed assistance – to leave, that is. It was obvious what Richard Hughes and all the other established trainers and owners were doing there. But two blokes from Dartford? Maybe it was just me, but horse ownership has always been associated with wealth and class, and it's only recently that 'ordinary people' have broken through, mainly via syndicates and clubs.

Mick, Patrick and Trevor were happy to let me and Pete represent the North South Syndicate. This was the rather unimaginative name we had picked for the group over our pint in the Old Wellington last week. Patrick and Mick live in York, the others in the Dartford and Bexleyheath area. We could have gone for something pompous and aspirational, or even vaguely witty, but settled instead for the literal. Two blokes from the North and three from the South. The North South Syndicate it was.

We were met with a fabulous sight when we reached the summit. The golden Pegasus weathervane flying proudly at the top of the hill was shining brightly in the autumn sun. Immediately to the right was a parade ring, similar in size to those found on racecourses. Yearlings were already being led round by lads and lasses whose love of working with these beautiful creatures makes the whole game possible. There were no saddles or number cloths to obscure the view of every young, equine body. In the warm, luminous light, they all looked magnificent, coats gleaming, the only blemish a small white sticker on their rear quarters displaying a lot number.

It wasn't long before we bumped into Jackie. Tom was elsewhere taking a look at some of the yearlings he had shortlisted on pedigree. I had done my homework as well. On the Tattersalls website the extended pedigree of every yearling was available. This was a useful starting point but much more work was needed. The pedigrees included only snippets of the dam's racing record and the performances of her other offspring. If you wanted to go deeper, and I did, then additional research using the Racing Post website was required.

I did the lot. I tried to pinpoint relatively unfashionable stallions whose offspring may be value for money, and also looked closely at newish ones who had promising statistics without being sensational and already in high demand. I tried to pinpoint dams who had been forward enough to win as two-year-olds and who had produced juvenile winners themselves. I looked up the racing records of such progeny, scribbled notes on the pedigrees printed-off from the Tattersalls on-line catalogue and turned up with a plastic wallet containing a dozen or so crumpled and annotated sheets of A4 paper which was effectively my shortlist.

The first yearling on the list was lot 1312, a light bay filly by the Group 1 winning sprinter, Equiano. The dam was Iridescence who had won twice as a three-year-old and whose only other foal to date, Raydiance, had won a seven-furlong listed race at Ascot and had a British Horseracing Authority (BHA) official rating in excess of 100. We would be delighted if we ended up with a horse rated 70-80 who was physically sound, mentally willing and able to be competitive in modest class 4 or 5 handicaps. This was one in which to take a keen interest

Exactly why this filly was in the Book 3 catalogue was a bit of a mystery to me. Tom had explained during our stable visit that only yearlings with the very best breeding ended up in the Book 1 sale. Apparently, Tattersalls reps also make visual inspections of many of the young horses, prior to cataloguing them, to confirm that they have the physique to match the pedigree. This was all news to me. I knew what the markets said and understood that we needed to buy from the Book 3 or even Book 4 sales in the hope that we could get something in our price range. But some of the yearlings on offer on that crisp October morning seemed to have pedigrees that would attract substantial bids. Perhaps the Tattersalls rep who visited this young Iridescence filly reckoned she failed on the leg-count score.

As she skipped round the paddock all four legs appeared to be present. Tom wasn't, though. He was somewhere in the stable complex scrutinising other yearlings. He was still elsewhere when the filly was brought into the sales ring and, as we were not authorised to bid, we watched on helplessly as the auction began. The bids soon exceeded our 10,000 guineas limit but to my surprise they stalled at 13,000 and the youngster was led out, unsold. It was early days, I thought. We needed to be patient although I recognised the importance of buying today to avoid the need of returning tomorrow for the second day of the sales. I hadn't prepared for that eventuality and all my pedigree research had focussed on lots for sale on day one. But there wasn't any need to panic at this point. I felt sure we'd pick up something soon.

Another few possibilities came and went. For one Swiss Spirit colt the bidding went into orbit ruling us out fairly quickly. For another, whose breeding I forget, Jackie observed that she was badly offset and not a good walker. This was not evident to my uneducated eye, but I was assured that although the yearling might make a nice riding horse, there were serious concerns about her ability to stand up to the rigours of training and racing.

Tom emerged from his travels and told us about one or two that he'd seen and liked which were worth considering. We were comparing notes when it was time for lot number 1383 to come into the ring. Jackie had run her eye over this filly in the paddock and liked her. She was a bit on the small side perhaps, but compact and we agreed this was one to go after.

Lot 1383 was an attractive bay filly by Equiano out of Peace And Love. She ticked plenty of boxes when I researched her pedigree last week. The sire, Equiano, was a Group 1 winning sprinter for Barry Hills, victorious in the Kings Stands Stakes at Royal Ascot in 2008 and 2010. As you would expect, he's an influence for speed and his most successful offspring is The Tin Man, a Group 1 winner over sprint distances. Like father, like son. Equiano also gets his fair share of two-year-old winners which was a plus as our syndicate couldn't afford a slow-burner making a racecourse debut at the back-end of the flat season by which time all our money would have gone up in smoke. We'd have loved to have the means to buy such a horse, but we didn't.

The dam was the dreamily named Peace And Love. She had won as a two-year-old and was pitched into listed company at York and Sandown, which I imagine were attempts to enhance her value as a broodmare, as much as anything. Being placed in a listed or group race is shown in extended pedigrees in bold, and owners are always keen for their fillies and mares to achieve 'black type'. There was no black type for Peace And Love and no further wins after her Kempton maiden victory in May 2005. She did, however, go to the breeding sheds as a winner and at her peak had a respectable BHA rating of 82.

More importantly, Peace And Love was now a proven broodmare. She had produced four previous foals. One was the result of mating with a minor American stallion, Conagree, who was based in Kentucky at the time. How that was arranged, I really don't know. Conagree Warrior ran three times without troubling the judge and that was the end of his racing career. Dimitar, a colt by another American stallion, Mizzen Mast, had more success, winning four races in 45 attempts, all at around a mile. His form tailed off towards the end of his career, but he won off a BHA rating of 69 and peaked at 75 at one point.

It was the other two relatives that really caught the eye. Rather unusually, lot number 1383 was a full-sister to two winning horses. It seems to me that most breeders avoid taking their mares back to the same stallion as by the time the younger brother or sister makes it to the sales ring, their older sibling may have proved themselves to be completely useless. Breeders like spreading the risk by pursuing variation. For lot number 1383 to be one of **three** full - brothers and sisters was unusual to say the least.

The older sister was Lydia's Place, winner of five of her 28 races, all at the minimum distance of five furlongs. She was clearly precocious and had rattled up a three-timer as a juvenile by early July. She won two more races and proved to be incredibly hardy and genuine, running 14 times as a four-year-old. Her highest BHA rating was 89 and, as she has not been sighted on the racecourse for a while, I can only guess that she has started her new career as a broodmare.

Lawless Louis was a year behind his big sister, and he won two from 16, both at the minimum distance. The apparent insistence on keeping him to five furlongs was a little strange, as he put up what was probably his best performance on one of only two occasions that he was tried over six furlongs. He finished a close sixth of 20 in the £100,000 two-year-old sales race at Redcar. Lawless Louis was also precocious, winning his two races early in his first season. He did train on though, running consistently well as a three-year-old including a close third to big sister Lydia's Place in a handicap at Beverley. His highest BHA rating was 84 and at the end of the 2017 flat season he was sold to race in Qatar.

Yes, I had slogged through this pedigree and many more before we rolled up full of hope on that glorious day in October. This was one that looked a potential early season type and with a winning full-brother and sister, the percentages were in our favour. Jackie liked the small bay filly with the lot 1383 sticker on her hind-quarters, and with Tom still looking at yearlings elsewhere, we asked her to bid on our behalf.

Pete and I positioned ourselves in the standing area at the mouth of the indoor sales ring. Through this entrance all the yearlings appeared, like actors taking the stage. And for a minute or two they had the limelight to themselves, walking around the periphery of a space about the size of a football pitch's centre circle. In the middle was a small carpet of straw arranged in an immaculate oval.

It was far from a full house. The seating which surrounded the ring, creating an amphitheatre, contained a scattering of people. The empty seats outnumbered the occupied ones by quite some margin. This sitting area was reserved for authorised bidders, but it didn't look like that to me. Perhaps that rule is more stringently applied for the Book 1 sales when all the big hitters are there and the actors on stage are by sires such as Galileo, Frankel and Dubawi. Nevertheless, we compliantly stood in our allotted area as lot 1383 brushed past us and began her stroll around the centre circle.

I don't have very clear memories of what happened next. The auctioneer's patter was rapid. I just remember snippets: 'By the group one winning sire Equiano…. winning full-brother and sister…. I've got five, who'll give me six?' The asking price steadily increased. The advancements weren't rapid and at around 8,000 guineas I thought we might have a chance. But soon the electronic board situated to my right, directly above the auctioneer's box, was showing 10,000 guineas which was our agreed limit. In one flicker it turned into 11,000 and we were out of the race.

I shrugged and told Pete that we'd just have to move on to the next one on the shortlist, as the neat bay filly left the sales ring via the exit directly opposite where we were standing. There would be no curtain call for us.

What I hadn't taken in, was that the yearling had been led away unsold. The owner must have put a slightly higher reserve price on his asset, and nobody had bid up to the amount he was looking for. The owner and breeder in question was Brendan Boyle, who had also bred and sold the full-brother and sister, Lawless Louis and Lydia's Place. Those two went quite cheaply at the sales but perhaps Brendan felt that as they had proved themselves on the racecourse winning seven races between them, the latest family relative would generate more interest and a bigger price.

Jackie came up to me as we were about to leave the ring to consider our next move and asked if we wanted to make a private offer to Brendan. It was only at this point that I realised that the filly hadn't been sold and we could do this. I remembered Tom telling me that plenty of deals were done in this way as many owners and breeders sometimes take less than they want for their stock as the alternative is paying for their keep for a few more months until the next suitable sale. Take a grand less now and avoid the cost of upkeep for a few more months to come.

Jackie quickly tracked down Brendan. He would be ready to shake on 10,500 guineas. However, Jackie playfully intimated that the last bid may well have been Brendan's as there were no other underbidders rushing to do business with him. There's nothing unusual or unethical about these tactics. In the end, buyers must pay what they feel a horse is worth, sticking to the financial limits they have set themselves. Fortunately, this was a straightforward bit of negotiating as there was no room for manoeuvre. All I had to do was state the facts.

'I'm not being funny Brendan, but I don't have any scope to bargain. There are five of us buying a horse for the first time and we've agreed on a 10,000 guineas limit for our purchase. That's all I can offer. We'll just move on to the next one on the shortlist if that's no good,' was my honest assessment of what we could do.

It was easy to say. Easier than haggling over the price of a car or a house because it was just a statement of fact and involved no bluffing or brinksmanship. It was very much a take it or leave it offer. I think Brendan realised that I had told it to him straight. We shook hands and the bay filly by Equiano out of Peace And Love, foaled 25 April 2016, became the property of the North South Syndicate.

You can do as much research as you like and if you have enough money to spread the net wide and buy lots of horses from different sales then I guess you'll end up with something that is really decent. Some will be completely useless. And you will almost certainly crack a wry smile at the oldest joke of them all. How do you make a small fortune out of owning racehorses? Start with a big fortune.

But when five of you have agreed to stump up £6,000 each for a once in a lifetime project, and you go with a strict budget to one day of one particular sale, you are very much at the mercy of the gods.

Would our purchase turn out to be a horse that would give the five of us lots of fun and perhaps prove capable of winning a little race? What about a big race! And what about the ones we missed? Lot 1312, the sprightly filly also by Equiano, was eventually sold privately for 14,000 guineas. If the bidding hadn't been so warm, maybe we would have ended up with her. And If I had taken a crystal ball to Newmarket that morning and stared intently at it, I would have glimpsed a future that revealed that we had experienced a near-miss. A year later, this other Equiano filly had made two racecourse appearances. Named Frequence, she was destined to finish last of eight beaten nearly 20 lengths in a minor event at Kempton and last of five in another minor contest at Brighton, beaten by a very similar margin. But I suppose she's still young and could improve. We all travel in hope.

Immediately after we had purchased our yearling filly, we made our way to the on-site restaurant to grab a light lunch with Tom and Jackie and talk through what happens next. Tom was going to let the filly settle down for a couple of weeks on a farm which he uses for horses who are not in full training. He explained about breaking her in and we chatted again about getting her ready to run early if that was possible. We quizzed Jackie about paperwork. There was so much to do but I could do most of it online with the BHA as soon as I registered as an owner and set up the North South Syndicate. Jackie would sort out the horse's passport and look into insurance for us, while the exciting stuff like choosing a name and racing colours could wait. Jackie advised looking into membership of the Racehorse Owners Association (ROA) which provided plenty of support for all types of owners, including absolute novices like us.

We didn't hang around after lunch to see how much other yearlings on our shortlist went for. I made a point of **not** following their progress as I couldn't bear finding out that we had narrowly missed buying a bargain-basement superstar. The die was cast, and it was best to concentrate on what we had.

Before leaving, it occurred to me that we should go and see our purchase. We knew what box number she occupied and as Tom and Jackie were staying all day in the hope of buying other yearlings, it was safe to assume that our filly wouldn't be put on a horsebox until much later. There were large maps of the stabling blocks located on building walls and despite the vast scale of the Tattersalls complex, we were able to find her after a fairly brief search.

According to the catalogue, our filly was located in Highflyer Paddock F. We peered into box 148 and there she was, turned away from us, quiet and showing little interest in her curious visitors. A young stable lad appeared.

'Is this yours?' he enquired in a soft Irish accent. I assumed he was with the Brendan Boyle team and was on watch duty, looking after a horse or two before they got picked up. As far as our yearling was concerned, this was the end of the story for him.

'Would you like me to get her out for you?'

We didn't need a second invitation. We would never have thought to ask, and to be presented with a chance of a picture taken holding our horse was just too good and too exciting to be true.

Our filly was led out by the stable lad and immediately gave a hint of the calm temperament with which she was blessed. She was placid and amenable, happy to stand quietly for her two much more excitable visitors. We took turns at holding her and posing for photographs, snapped on our mobile phones. Doing this meant that we were the *real* owners of this filly. Not one of about 20 who had most of the organisation done for them by a racing club or syndicate manager. This was *our* horse. We had bought her, we would name her, we would choose her racing colours, and we would visit the stable whenever we wanted to discuss with our trainer what races we could target. This was the real deal.

That picture of me holding our gorgeous bay filly is one of my most prized possessions. It only exists as a digital image. I haven't reproduced it and had it professionally framed or arranged for it to be emblazoned on a t-shirt. It's good enough to know that it happened on that fabulous October day and the image is permanent, inviolable, even if only in my mind's eye.

16 October 2017

It was time to get stuck into the admin. My personal circumstances made it relatively easy to devote time to tasks such as registering our syndicate with the BHA, setting up a racing bank account with Weatherbys, getting my head around VAT registration and disseminating information and updates to the others via email or the 'Peace and Love' WhatsApp group that we set up. I had retired from primary school headship in April 2017 and for years beforehand had thought, that when I finished, I would like to buy a horse. The theory was that at this point in my life I would have the time and money to take on this project.

I had experienced ownership before. My penny shares (typically 5%) of various horses sourced by the Heart of the South Racing club made for a great introduction to the thrill of ownership. Clear Daylight, a strapping son of Daylami trained by John Best in Kent, was my first involvement. I split the cost of the share with Trevor. Due to work commitments I couldn't make his first two runs at Newmarket and Goodwood. Being the Head Teacher of Hurst Primary School meant slipping off early to go and watch my horse run wasn't possible. Well possible, but unimaginable.

The children at Hurst are friendly, good-natured and polite, but they are children after all, and you could bet your last fiver that something would go dreadfully wrong. It would be one of those days when two of my more hot-headed boys would get overly competitive in their football match during afternoon break. One would end up needing a precautionary visit to A&E leaving my excellent Deputy, Jayne, to deal with irate parents who demanded to see the head. Unfortunately, he wasn't available. He was at Goodwood. No, sneaking out, even just a few minutes early, wasn't an option.

I made it to Lingfield though for Clear Daylight's third run which fell in the half-term break. I can still remember the buzz of being in the middle of the parade ring with the other owners waiting for our jockey to join us and receive his briefing from the trainer.

The race itself was soon in danger of becoming a disaster with our boy looking distinctly uneasy around the sharp Lingfield bends. He was well behind but made some late, moderately encouraging headway in the short straight to get within six lengths of the winner, albeit in tenth place. The official Racing Post comment read: *Slowly into stride, detached in last, reminder over 2f out and over 1f out, kept on, never a factor.* The jockey was Stephane Breux, who rode a handful of winners in England before returning to France where he is still working but struggling to pick up rides as far as I can see. Stephane said he was pleased with Clear Daylight's late progress and felt the horse would be better over further and on a more galloping track. Stephane's English was good, but I couldn't help thinking that his observation needed no translation. The language was international. 'He's pretty slow, so you might as well throw him over a longer trip and see what happens.'

Clear Daylight was now handicapped, having had his three qualifying runs, and the next stop was Kempton on 7 November 2007 for the class 6 Dgibet Nursery Handicap over a mile. We had been allocated an official BHA rating of 64. To this day I can still remember how fabulous he looked in the paddock. It was early November, but his coat was gleaming and he appeared to be in great shape. John Best said that we had an each-way chance and it certainly looked that way just judging by appearances.

Clear Daylight was ridden by the experienced Dane O'Neil who settled him in midfield. The partnership was still going well when the tightly grouped field turned for home. At the two-furlong marker, Dane shook the reins and started pushing. Clear Daylight's response was immediate. At the furlong-pole we may have even hit the front and the owners were in full voice. But, just as an unlikely victory seemed on the verge of unfolding, Clear Daylight's head came up, he drifted to the right and was squeezed up slightly before finishing fifth to the well backed favourite. It was from exhilaration to crushing disappointment in seconds.

I raced down the grandstand steps, easy to do at Kempton's winter twilight meetings, which are often very poorly attended, and managed to catch our jockey before he disappeared into the warmth of the weighing room. Dane offered, rather unconvincingly, that the horse may have been spooked by the big screen on the inside of the track, but I felt he was being generous. It looked like Clear Daylight had the pace to win it but didn't know what to do once he got to the front. It could have been a bit of inexperience but for all their breeding and training, racehorses remain pack animals and some of them just like running around with the others.

The rest of the story is dull and predictable. We stayed with the Clear Daylight partnership for another season, but he didn't win a race or even creep into the first four which would have meant a tiny bit of prize money. He only had three more races after Kempton and, following a few niggling physical problems, it was agreed that he should go to the October horses in training sale. With a very modest BHA rating of 55 and a thoroughly uninspiring racing record, it was no surprise that he fetched a mere 800 guineas. I still have the uncashed cheque from Heart of the South for £5.85 which was our share of the sale proceeds once all administration and transport costs had been deducted. As for the horse, apparently a farmer in Kent who breeds heavy horses felt that Clear Daylight might make a good stallion. Talk about rewarding failure!

I had a number of other small shares in horses with Heart of the South during the next ten years. Some were good – South Cape, The Shuffler, Good Luck Charm. Some were total flops like Clear Daylight. But I loved the experience. It introduced me to stable visits, watching the horses work on the gallops, and contact with trainers and jockeys. It opened up the fascinating behind the scenes side of racing to me. It also made me even more aware of the high levels of care and affection shown to horses by those who work with them on a daily basis. We love our horses. We become emotionally attached to them. The first thing that any owner with a shred of integrity wants, even before the stalls open and the race begins, is that their horse comes back safe and well. And when their racing days are over, we want the best possible homes for them. The horse always comes first. It's the only way to justify our sport, and its long-term survival depends on everyone committing to the highest possible levels of animal welfare in what will always be an activity full of peril, only fit for the bold, the brave and the compassionate.,

Those were my penny share experiences. Some of them were fabulous. I've been in the winners' enclosure a few times and remember with great fondness the first time that happened when The Shuffler bolted up in a very modest classified stakes at Brighton, which was for horses rated no higher than 55. It didn't matter that it was a weak race and the prize money would barely cover a month's training fees. Our boy won! Is there really a feeling like it? It was The Shuffler's first win after nine attempts and although he was to go on and race five more times, notching up another win in the process, Brighton felt like a fulfilling conclusion. The result was in the official form book, a permanent mark that couldn't be erased. I was there and part of it.

1 November 2017

Today's job was to register the partnership which involved paying a fee from the Weatherbys bank account which I had set up a few days ago. Everything seemed to involve a fee. I had calculated that our collective fund of £30,000 would take us until the end of July, after which we would have to top up the account if our filly had failed to win any prize money. Although I secretly yearned for her to be one of those once-in-a-lifetime bargain-basement superstars, I knew that very many horses don't even make it to the racecourse. If they do, it's for a handful of uninspiring runs before it's accepted that they're not going to make the grade. I forget who it was, but I remember that a trainer once observed that about a third of all horses have too many ongoing physical problems to stand up to racing, another third are no good or not interested, and it's only from the final third that you have a chance of unearthing a winner. My consistent line to the boys was to accept that we could get to the middle of the season only to discover that the filly we bought was not a racing proposition and she had no residual value either. It would then be a case of finding a good home for her while accepting that we had each become £6-7k poorer. Looking on the gloomiest side is the only way to approach ownership – while at the same time harbouring unrealistic hopes of having bought a champion for buttons. Doublethink is a useful skill for all owners to possess. How did George Orwell describe doublethink in 1984? *The power of holding two contradictory beliefs in one's mind simultaneously, and accepting both of them.* That sums up racehorse ownership in a nutshell.

How we arrived at the £6,000 figure that we would put into the fighting fund was dictated by personal circumstances and an acceptance that this would be a time-limited partnership. We would run it for a year and send our filly to the autumn horses in training sale unless we all agreed on another course of action. I wouldn't describe any of the five of us as being rich but that's relative. We're rich enough to think about buying a horse rather than worry about where the next rent payment will come from. We've all got our own financial priorities and plans for the future, and like everyone in a partnership, some of us had to consider more than others how much the family budget could withstand. If it was a choice between a completely refurbished bathroom and a precocious sprint-bred yearling, I'm not sure if my wife, Jennie, would have spent too long weighing up the options. I don't think that the winning full-brother and full-sister blurb would have swayed the argument.

Don't get me wrong, Jennie is a star. She actually enjoys going racing, especially if it's somewhere that has a bit of style. Sandown is her favourite track, but we've had lovely days out at Windsor, the Newmarket July course, Goodwood and the dearly departed and much missed Folkestone. She really loves horses as well and has enjoyed seeing them in the flesh at Gary Moore and Tom Clover's stables. She just thinks I'm a bit obsessed with it all.

'What are you looking at now?' is a typical enquiry from my better half.

'Just reading the news on the Racing Post app,' is my usual reply.

'You're obsessed with that! You're always looking at it. I really don't know how much time you spend every day looking at horses, but it must be hours.'

That's a bit of an exaggeration, but maybe only a bit. I can't let it go unchallenged though. I have to mount some sort of defence.

'That's rich!' I sometimes counter if feeling brave. 'You spend hours fiddling with your phone on Facebook. You don't realise how much time you're spending on it.'

'Rubbish! I just check the news to keep in touch with friends which is a social activity. What you're doing is solitary and obsessive. You get lost in it.'

There's no answer to that. A small sigh indicating that I am totally misunderstood is all that I can usually muster. Obsessed? That's a bit strong. Totally consumed by this horse buying project and horse racing in general, I admit. But obsessed?

You know how it is, though. By way of illustration, I remember doing a bit of study before the last flat meeting of the season at Sandown. I was on the Racing Post website where it's so easy to get lost, to disappear dream-like into another world. I noted a John Gosden two-year-old making its debut in the novice race. It was a colt by Redoute's Choice, an Australian stallion about which I knew very little. I did a bit of research and found out that in 2014 he was standing in France and had a whopping stud fee of 60,000 euros. His race record was impressive, winning four out of eight and all of these wins were at grade 1 level, from six furlongs to a mile. I hadn't taken note of his exploits at the time, but he was clearly a seriously fast and classy animal who was in action on the Australian racing scene at the turn of the millennium. I dug deeper. His stock sell for big money and he's sired grade 1 winners. He's not just an influence for speed and, rather surprisingly, the average winning distance of his progeny is 9.4 furlongs.

The dam of this young John Gosden debutant was Sevanna, a useful staying filly by the great Galileo. She managed to win a group 3 race at Goodwood for the late and much-loved Sir Henry Cecil. I clicked on the date of that 2009 Lily Langtry Stakes at Goodwood and watched a video replay of Sevanna in action. I could have watched all of her races if I really wanted to, before looking at the exploits of her other offspring. I did the latter and noted that the three sons and daughters to date - Savanne, Sassella and Samurai - had all won races at 10-12 furlongs and were all smart racehorses. I looked them up and discovered that Savanne won at group 3 level in France and Sassella was successful in listed class.

If the youngster making his racecourse debut at Sandown had inherited any of the family's ability, then he may have a bright future ahead of him. This was definitely one to watch because it's all about the possibility of what he might become. Could Sevanna Star show at Sandown that he was a group horse in the making? A Derby horse? Could he show enough to get people dreaming?

He was one of four young horses making their debuts in this class 5 novice event on a quiet Wednesday towards the end of the season. I looked at my watch and noted that nearly half an hour of my life had just vanished, disappeared into an imagined and uncertain future, where disappointments heavily outweigh the exhilaration of success. Obsessed? I prefer passionately engaged, which sounds much more endearing.

Lot 1383, the bay yearling filly by Equiano out of Peace And Love, at Tattersalls before entering the sales ring.

3 The Naming Game

2 November 2017

The most exciting thing about the admin was undoubtedly sorting out a name for our filly. This was something that needed to be done through the Holborn based BHA. It's hard when you have five opinions and possibly as many suggestions to deal with but at least it was just the five of us. I'm sure every owner wants a good name for their horse, but if you buy an older one, you have no choice. You have to take what you're given. That's one of the exciting things about buying a yearling. It's unraced, not yet named, and fantasising about the endless possibilities for its future is more than half the fun.

Nobody wants a bad name for their pride and joy, and I remembered an old racing adage about not being able to win the Epsom Derby with a poorly named horse. It is true that there have been some magnificently named Derby winners. Hyperion, Nijinksy, Troy and Galileo are just a handful whose names conjure up images of heroism and greatness. But there was also the 1818 winner, Sam. Perhaps he was the exception that proved the rule.

I suppose Sam is ordinary rather than hopping lame. I can recall some dreadfully named horses running around British racetracks over the last five decades. One that stands out was a creature named Plastic Cup. What possesses anyone to saddle a horse with a moniker like that? It's a crushing burden for a thoroughbred to carry. Needless to say, Plastic Cup did not win the Epsom Derby. Other names I am not too keen on are those that put three or four words together without spaces to conform with the rule that a racehorse's name must be no longer than 18, characters including spaces. This means we get animals such as Didntcostalotbut, a conspicuously unsuccessful hurdler in the early noughties. I'm sure his owners loved him dearly and forgave him for the dismal efforts in the only three races he managed, but that type of name doesn't really do it for me. It courts mediocrity.

I remember when Heart of the South got in touch with me and the other 19 owners of the Reset yearling that had just been syndicated and needed a name. He was a homebred, the dam being Lucky Dice who was owned by the Penny family. Every shareholder was entitled to a suggestion. Once they were received, they were made known to all of the owners who then had to vote for their favourite. I suppose all 20 could have put an X beside their own choice producing a bizarre stalemate. But that didn't happen and 'The Shuffler' was chosen as the name for our colt.

Of course, the subtlety of this name was lost on most. As the dam was Lucky Dice, somebody thought it was either witty or appropriate (perhaps both) to refer to games of chance. The Croupier would have been good. The Dealer even better but almost certainly unavailable as I recall the Lambourn maestro Fred Winter training a very useful jumper by that name in the 1970s. In the end, The Shuffler it was, and sharing this information with family and friends invariably prompted guffaws and gasps of consternation.

'The Shuffler? The Shuffler? What possessed you to give a racehorse that name? Is he arthritic?'

I should have made a digital recording on my mobile so when confronted with this predictable question, I could just press a button and out would flow an explanation of the name. The need to cut through hysterical laughter with my increasingly robotic and weary response, became quite tiresome. As I have mentioned, The Shuffler proved to be a bonny little horse winning two races but every time he ran down the field, I was reminded that I was asking for it, giving a racehorse such a ridiculous name.

Names matter. They don't make horses run any faster, but I have a suspicion that they could make them even slower. Our little filly's name needed to inspire pride, hope and joy, not ridicule and public shame. The naming of our yearling was a task to be taken seriously.

4 November 2017

After all the saving, planning and deliberations, things started to move pretty quickly. Tom had set up another WhatsApp group and before 9am we all received 14 seconds of video footage of our filly being broken in. Tom was gently leading her on a lunge rein around a circular paddock enclosed by leafy laurel trees. In the accompanying message he told us that the filly was coming along nicely. She was doing everything asked of her and looked quite strong despite her relatively small size. Tom told us that she would start to be ridden next week. It was fantastic to receive updates in this way. Our trainer clearly understood the value of communication with owners and, being relatively young, it was no surprise that he was comfortable with using digital communication for everyone's benefit. It occurred to me that I needed to crack on with the admin.

7 November 2017

More evidence shortly arrived that I needed need to get into gear with the paperwork. Tom sent another early morning video via the WhatsApp group:

Morning all. Here is your filly this morning. It was the first day ridden away. As you can see, she looks strong.

The new clip showed our little filly (and she did look quite small) happily trotting around the circular paddock, unfussed by the presence of her rider who gently bobbed up and down in the saddle. You could hear Tom's encouraging words and clicking noises which our girl responded to, flicking her ears in this direction and that. What a lovely sight it was. And what a great insight into how young horses are prepared for the business of training and racing.

8 November 2017

Another video clip arrived. Tom's message forewarned us that these videos wouldn't be so frequent from now on, which was understandable. As a new trainer at the start of his career, Tom didn't have hundreds of horses in his care, but he did have 25 which meant the Wroughton House yard he was renting was full and he had plenty of other owners to look after. This morning's video was 18 seconds long and showed our filly having her first day on Newmarket Heath. She was trotting around the large railed paddock which is situated at the foot of the gallops. Mick was quick to respond: *Lovely to see. Precious memories to keep. Thanks Tom.*

I hadn't met Mick before we launched our horse project. He was a friend of Patrick's and the other half of the York axis. Now retired, he was a postman whose delivery round included Patrick's house. When Patrick was relocated by the civil service to Leeds it didn't take him long to relocate himself again to York. It wasn't the greatest surprise to learn that the house he bought was a decent five iron away from the two-mile start of York racecourse. I'm not too sure exactly how Mick and Patrick struck up a friendship, but I know it was through racing. I imagine the conversation went something like this:

Mick: Morning. Just need your signature for this package please.
Pat: There you go. Fancy anything at York today?
Mick: You're interested in racing then?
Pat: I most certainly am.

Mick: Fancy buying a racehorse?
Pat: What a great idea!

Maybe there was bit more to it than that. Patrick and Mick are both sociable but undemonstrative types, so I think the conversation probably evolved over a number of years. All I know is that they got to know each other through horseracing and when we were planning our ownership project Patrick said that he had somebody in mind who might want to be part of the group.

I got to know Mick pretty well during our adventure. You'd be hard pressed to meet a more sincere and modest man. Owning a racehorse was 'living the dream' as far as Mick was concerned and his comments on our group app couldn't disguise how much he was enthralled by the whole experience - a man after my own heart.

16 November 2017

During the morning I received confirmation from the BHA that our syndicate registration had been approved. We were up and running and ready to tackle the first important job of naming our filly.

This was a surprisingly easy task. We didn't have lots of different suggestions with syndicate members arguing passionately for their particular cause. On the way back from last month's sales, Pete and I stopped off in a quiet village pub somewhere near Saffron Walden. We discussed names over a pint and were both keen to use the pedigree as our starting point.

Our filly's sire, Equiano, was named after a real person, Olaudah Equiano. Olaudah was an extraordinary man. He was a black African slave who was kidnapped with his sister at the age of 11, sold by local slave traders and shipped across the Atlantic to Barbados and then Virginia. In Virginia he was sold to a Royal Navy officer which meant that Olaudah travelled the oceans for eight years, during which time he was baptised and learned to read and write. He ended up in London where in 1789 he published his autobiography, *'The Interesting Narrative of the Life of Olaudah Equiano, the African'*. He travelled widely, promoting the book and the anti-slavery cause. He was part of the Sons of Africa, an abolitionist group composed of well-known Africans living in England and was also active in the anti-slave trade movement headed by William Wilberforce. Olaudah Equiano was a remarkable human being.

That was the dad. Our filly's mum was Peace And Love. There is no lengthy explanation required here. Peace And Love was by Fantastic Light out of Muschana so I can only assume that her owner just fancied the name or perhaps had a yearning for the hippy era. We came up with a couple of possibilities: Free Love and Slave To Love. We favoured the former fearing that the latter might produce a Twitterstorm of outrage despite its witticism. Free Love nodded to both sides of the pedigree and Pete and I agreed that it should definitely be on the shortlist. If ever proof were needed that fools seldom differ, a day or two later Patrick emailed his suggestion of Free Love which he had arrived at independently. When this suggestion was put to Mick and Trevor, we achieved a unanimous decision with the minimum of fuss.

17 November 2017

Holborn, we have a problem. The name Free Love came up as unavailable when I did my research on the BHA website. This surprised me as according to the Racing Post the only other horse in living memory to be named Free Love was a South African mare foaled in 1999. She won two small races before going off the racing radar. She couldn't have been used as a broodmare as there were no little sons and daughters of Free Love running around provincial tracks somewhere south of the equator.

Rather predictably, Slave To Love was available so I put a half-hearted reserve on it. I had no real enthusiasm for this alternative. It did nod to both sides of the pedigree, was passably witty, and as Bryan Ferry songs go, not too desperate. But all I could see in my crystal ball was a weary figure explaining to a series of stern faces and arched eyebrows that the origins of the filly's name were to be found in what her mum and dad were called. The accusation would be that the name was disrespectful to the memory of a revered anti-slavery campaigner, and possibly downright offensive.

Of course, it would be none of these things and perhaps my imagination was running away with me. Would Slave To Love really cause such a storm if she made her debut in a class 5 novice event at Southwell? That particular track holds the unenviable record of the lowest paying attendance on any one day at a British racecourse. It was thirteen, unlucky for some. But perhaps the name might cause a ripple if we bolted up in the Queen Mary Stakes at Royal Ascot in June and ended up being ante-post favourite for the following year's 1,000 Guineas. It was on that basis that I decided Slave To Love was unusable.

18 November 2017

Another video clip arrived from Tom. Under blue winter skies on Newmarket Heath, it showed a string of six horses cantering very steadily in single file. It looked like Jackie Jarvis was riding Free Love. Tom's message confirmed that our filly was now doing regular steady canters and was, 'Coming along nicely.' Everything was going according to plan and it struck me that we might be only a shade over four months away from making our racecourse debut. Better sort out a name quickly.

20 November 2017

Patrick sent me a message telling me that the name Free Love was available last time he checked. His news arrived via email rather than through the WhatsApp group. Over the years it had become apparent that Patrick and smartphones were not things that you were likely to spot together. If you wanted to get in touch with him, you could try a number of strategies. First and most reliable was the landline. However, this often meant leaving a message which would be ignored, but at least you heard his voice telling you that he wasn't available. Email was always worth a try but it usually needed a seven-day turnaround. You'd be better off sending a handwritten letter. For those with unshakeable optimism, ringing Patrick's ancient mobile phone was worth a punt but your call being picked up was realistically priced at 33/1. It was 50/1 that your text message would receive a reply. I'm not sure whether Patrick really owned a working mobile phone. At times, I thought he had given me a random set of numbers to keep me happy and provide the illusion that I could get in touch with him.

I replied promptly to Patrick, informing him that I had used the BHA name checker and Free Love was coming up as currently unavailable. However, I said that I'd speak to someone at the BHA and confirm whether or not this was the case

My email message concluded with the usual pleasantries including, GET A BLOODY SMARTPHONE, PATRICK!

21 November 2017

The BHA website is a great place to lose hours of your life. I was beginning to get to grips with it and soon became hooked on using the search facility for future races. I was able to use a whole range of filters to identify targets for two-year-fillies. I could see everything for which we were eligible, ranging from class 6 races at Musselburgh worth £3,000 to the winner, to the prestigious Royal Ascot group races worth more than twenty times that amount. I found out that I could filter by track, by trip, by race value, and so on. You name it, I could do it. I was probably doing a bit too much searching as my intention to contact the BHA and make a personal enquiry about our filly's name completely slipped my mind for an hour or so. I finally remembered and was quickly put through to somebody who deals with the naming of horses.

There are plenty of rules governing the naming of horses other than stipulating how many characters and spaces you can have. You are not allowed anything rude or offensive. So how Mary Hinge and Duckey Fuzz slipped through the net is anybody's guess. You can't choose the name of a real person until 50 years after their death. For somebody still in the land of the living, you need their written permission. References to political parties and allegiances are also banned so Fascist Dictator and Socialist Workers Party Lad (too many characters anyway) would also go by the wayside.

My enquiry was a simple one. I just needed confirmation that Free Love was definitely unavailable. If that was the case, we'd have to have a serious rethink. The very helpful member of staff assured me that she could make a check and give me an answer right away. She informed me that there was indeed a Free Love registered as a mare, but it didn't look as if she had been active and, in any event, it was now just over twenty years since her naming. I was told that there was no reason why we couldn't have this name. All the BHA staff member had to do was click a button to free it up. All I had to do was go back to the website and put a reserve on Free Love.

Bingo! The 'name available' message popped up and with a single confirming click, our Equiano filly had a name. It was all coming together. We had a horse, we had a name, we had a trainer, we had evidence of the early breaking-in and training regimes going to plan. All that lay ahead now was a winter of unbearable waiting.

4 In The Beginning

22 November 2017

Despite Tom's warning that the WhatsApp video updates would be less frequent, we still received them on an impressively regular basis. Newmarket Heath looked and sounded a very different place in the next 18 second clip provided. Tom's accompanying message told us that we were watching Free Love having her second day cantering on the grass and that she was finding it all very easy. The video showed a much bigger, older looking horse leading the small group of five, again in single file. The canter was steady and carried out against a pewter sky and a row of trees on the verge of surrendering their last fiery-red leaves. But it was the noise that caught my attention. You would have thought Tom was at sea. The raw and blustery wind conveyed the openness and wildness of the heath. It sounded as if the sails of a boat were being unfurled and battered by a gale. As the very depths of winter approached, men and women whose lives revolve around the care of racehorses were out there in the wild. And one of them was even trying to capture the moment on a mobile phone for the benefit of owners tucked up in their suburban warmth.

30 November 2017

We received another video bulletin via our newly named 'Free Love' WhatsApp group. The Heath was calmer but now there was frost on the grass that bordered the uphill all-weather gallop. As before, it was only a gentle canter, but Tom's message revealed that things were progressing well and he intended to give Free Love a couple of half-speed pieces of work before Christmas.

Spring couldn't come soon enough. There were so many hurdles still to cross and no indication as yet about Free Love's ability. All we knew was that she had taken the early stuff in her stride. Her temperament seemed sound enough at this point, but whether she could run fast enough, or even *want* to run fast, were other matters.

Another reason for wishing the winter away was my association of the spring and summer with the flat season. Although I really enjoy the spectacle of jump racing, my heart belongs to the flat. That may seem a little strange given that my first proper equine hero was the mighty Sea Pigeon. Hero is the right word. I idolised the horse and for six or seven years couldn't allow Sea Pigeon to race without a small amount of my money riding on his handsome dark brown back. He was a mercurial talent in his early days. Good enough to finish seventh in Morston's 1973 Derby, but also disappointing enough on other occasions to be deemed temperamental and possibly ungenuine.

I was not remotely interested in horse racing at the time of the 1973 Epsom Derby. In fact, whenever I saw racing on the television it was a cue to switch channels and find something else to watch. I joined the Sea Pigeon story in the autumn of 1974, shortly after my engagement with the sport began. Sea Pigeon had now been gelded and sold to Pat Muldoon whose Macintyre tartan colours were worn by the great horse's jockeys for the rest of his racing career.

Sea Pigeon appealed to me on two counts. Clearly, he was talented, but he had not fulfilled his considerable potential. Perhaps it was there still waiting to be unlocked. Secondly, and more importantly, he developed a thrilling racing style which involved being held up off the pace before being produced with a scything late run. There's nothing better in horseracing than seeing a class act surge past the opposition late on to seal a famous victory.

For the majority of his career Sea Pigeon was trained in Yorkshire by Peter Easterby and ridden by the popular Irishman Jonjo O'Neil. I was there at the 1981 Cheltenham Festival when under a masterful ride from John Francome, replacing the injured Jonjo, Sea Pigeon jumped the last in fourth place only for his jockey to wait until the final hundred yards to pounce and secure the horse's second Champion Hurdle victory. The place erupted and I ran to the winners' enclosure. More accurately, I pushed, shoved and wriggled my way to as near as I could to the paddock where the champion came in. I don't think I got very close, but I remember catching glimpses of the jubilation down below. I was there.

At eleven, Sea Pigeon had become the oldest Champion Hurdler in the race's history. Prior to that, he had revived his flat racing career winning two Chester Cups and an Ebor Handicap carrying ten stone to victory in the latter, which is still a record. He wasn't just popular in Yorkshire or with jumping aficionados. He was *loved* - I don't believe that's too strong a word - by the race-going public. I adored Sea Pigeon. I know I have seen better horses subsequently – not many hurdlers, mind – but there will only ever be one Sea Pigeon.

But I don't think I could get involved in owning a jumper. Injury and fatality rates are so much higher than on the flat and I unwittingly experienced this dark side of racing with one of my 'penny share' horses, Mr Spiggott. I have absolutely no doubt about the high levels of care that are shown by all staff in the racing industry to the horses in their charge. I also know that owners, trainers, stable staff and all connected with racehorses are absolutely devastated by a fatality which could take place on the gallops, at the races or through illness. It happened to me with Mr Spiggott and the only saving grace was that I wasn't able to be at Plumpton on 2 December 2013 because of work commitments.

Mr Spiggott had been owned by Doctor Marwan Koukash who has scores of horses in training and every year sells off some of his lesser lights. Heart of the South Racing obviously thought Mr

Spiggott was worth buying and syndicating. I took a 5% share and split it with Trevor and Derek.

Mr Spiggott disappointed for his new trainer, Joe Tuite, and even a change of scenery with Gary Moore didn't lead to a significant revival in form. Gary trains lots of jumpers and felt it was worth schooling Mr Spiggott over hurdles, and so I ended up with a National Hunt horse.

His Plumpton debut in November was a respectable third behind a young horse really going places, Regal Encore. With that positive experience under the horse's belt we were really hopeful of going even closer on that fateful December afternoon. I'll spare you the details. All I'll say is that our boy was jumping well in second place and enjoying himself when he stumbled and broke his near-fore leg a couple of strides before the third-last hurdle. Joshua Moore immediately jumped off his stricken partner. It was not long before the screens were up and the vet was on the scene to humanely put down poor Mr Spiggott.

As I wasn't there, Eloise Penny phoned me in person to communicate the grim news. I think Trevor had already got in touch from the course. It was sad enough for me, but what about the stable lad or lass who looked after Mr Spiggott on a daily basis and would have regarded the horse as their own? It was a dismal day and a reminder of why I prefer the flat.

When much younger, I remember the sickening feeling somewhere deep in my bowels when Sea Pigeon was caught by a swinging hurdle at Newbury and came crashing down. For an agonising second or two, the great horse seemed to roll in slow motion before clambering unsteadily to his feet and cantering away. It was only at that point that I knew he was safe. My sense of relief was palpable.

I can't remember how old I was at the time of that Newbury fall, but know that when I started following Sea Pigeon in the autumn of 1974, it was my first year in sixth-form. I was sixteen and becoming more and more engrossed with a sport which has captured my imagination for the best part of 45 years.

Looking back, it was a casual twist of fate that prompted my initial interest in racing. There was no helping hand from my family. My mum was a practical woman who hailed from Cork. She had come to London in search of work and a better life when she was just 21 and stayed ever since, showing very little sentimentality for the homeland thereafter. We were not, therefore, regular visitors to Ireland where I am sure I would have bumped into uncles, aunts and cousins who were caught up with horses. All of Ireland seems to be. As far as mum was concerned, 'A fool and his money are easily parted,' and she saw no reason why people would want to race horses against each other to find out which one was the fastest, let alone waste money by betting on the outcome as well. I only wish I had persuaded her to come as my guest to Sandown Park one summer when she was fit and well enough to do so. I'm sure she would have been pleasantly surprised and impressed by the elegance of the place. Not like Brighton Rock at all.

Although my grandfather liked a few bob on the horses every Saturday, following Lester Piggott and runners with the word 'silver' in their names, his weekly habit was not passed on to my dad. True, dad organised the annual each-way bets on the Grand National for me and my two brothers. Beyond that, the only other times I heard him mention horseracing was to warn against the excesses of gambling. It is therefore ironic that it was dad who introduced me to the world of racing, but in a very roundabout way.

Thomas Linnett, or 'Tommy' as he was always known to my mum, worked for the big UK construction and civil engineering company, McAlpine. He was not a qualified engineer. I got the impression that he would have liked to go down that route and I think he was bright enough to do so, but my grandfather worked for McAlpine and was able to secure a job for his son as soon as he reached school leaving age. Dad therefore left school without progressing to the type of further education and training required of engineers. He wasn't bitter about it. He had a good job and ended up being site manager on various projects including the construction of the Glasgow dry docks in the 1960s. My early primary school memories are of Newcastle-upon-Tyne, where I was born, and Glasgow.

In 1968 Dad was employed by John Howard and we made a permanent move to the South East. My parents looked for a location that would be a suitable, permanent family base. Being near to catholic schools and churches was top of the list and it was Sidcup that ticked all the boxes. Sidcup might not tick everybody's box, but it did for my parents whose prime concern was for their children's education and family life in general. There would be no more moving, regardless of where my dad was working. Which was just as well, because with the removal van barely unloaded, dad was asked to work on the huge and prestigious Humber Bridge project.

Tommy Linnett's latest construction job meant that I spent six weeks in either Barton (south of the river Humber) or Hessle (north) in the school summer holidays during my early teenage years. Outside this holiday period, my dad's weekly regime was brutal. He would arrive home at about 1pm every Saturday, having made a brief visit to the bridge construction site before driving south to Sidcup. At 4am on Monday he was on the road heading back to Hull. My poor mum was left to run the house and look after the three boys on her own, which wasn't the easiest of shifts.

There was some relief when the schools broke up at the end of the academic year. John Howard paid for a rented property during the summer holiday period. I can't remember too much about the houses in which we stayed. I seem to recall that they were modest, but clean and comfortable three-bedroom semis and it meant that the family could be together for a decent stretch of time during the summer. The children had no trouble finding things to do. Having three boys close together must have been hard work for mum but at least we had company and were able to amuse ourselves.

The Humber Bridge project was huge. I'm not sure how many summers we spent on the industrial banks of the Humber, but it must have been three or four. As we got older, my mum and dad thought it would be good if we could find some part-time local work. It would mean we could use our own cash to buy sweets and fritter away money in the penny arcades. As was the case in those days with firms like John Howard, it was deemed a perfectly reasonable piece of support to provide a holiday house for the site manager and his family, and also sort out some low-paid part-time work for his children. I think it was seen as looking after staff who for the bulk of the year lived lonely lives away from home. It should also be remembered that McAlpine and John Howard were very much family firms run by family members who understood how important looking after family was. And so, at the age of sixteen, a few weeks after finishing my O Level exams, I became assistant to the storekeeper on the Barton site of the Humber Bridge project.

Gordon Chester was the unfailingly cheerful and optimistic storekeeper who took me under his wing. I suppose Gordon was about 40 and he had come from a merchant navy background. I think I can remember a hint of a west country accent (Bristol perhaps?) and he definitely had an impressive and well-kept dark brown beard that gave him a nautical air. This was reinforced by the frequent singing of sea shanties and other songs from an extensive and remarkably clean catalogue. I have very fond memories of Gordon who showed me the ropes in the stores and taught me enough to be of vague use to the men who rolled up looking to book out a CP9 drill or a sledgehammer or two.

Lunchtimes meant form study for Gordon. He would puff on his pipe, hum away and pore over the Daily Mirror racing pages. The ritual invariably ended with somebody coming to collect his modest bets which would be taken to a local bookmaker. I became intrigued. What exactly was Gordon looking at? How did he decide which horses to back? What did all the figures and letters besides the names of the horses mean? Gordon was patient and only too happy to let me into his little world. I can't remember how much knowledge of the turf he actually possessed, but I had a bit of fun looking at the racing pages and picking out a few horses then looking up the results the next day to see how they got on. I didn't have a bet but enjoyed the fun of trying to pick winners and Gordon took an interest in how I was doing. I think it developed into an informal tipping competition.

And that was that. I was on my way thanks to a chance meeting in a part-time job on the banks of the river Humber. Through such events our lives are changed forever.

On returning to sixth-form after the summer break, I was made aware that one of the other students, Brian McElhinney, was interested in horse racing. I didn't know Brian very well despite the fact that our school, St Mary's in Sidcup, was a very small Catholic grammar school which was only two-form entry. Classes were either 'Alpha' or 'A'. Up until our O Level year I was in 5 Alpha and Brian in 5 A. You'd think with only two classes in each year everybody would get to know each other, but that wasn't the case. We were all timetabled along A and Alpha lines, so it was possible to spend five years in the same school, in the same small year group and not really get to know the thirty boys who inhabited the classroom next door. Now back in the sixth-form, we were all thrown together by A level subjects, not forms.

When I found out at the beginning of the academic year that Brian and his family were into racing, I got chatting with him about this shared interest. Very shortly we had devised our own tipping championship which ran for a whole flat or jump season and involved making daily selections and calculating profits and losses on the basis of the horses' starting prices. We even 'phoned each other on Saturday mornings to make our selections which I recorded in a pilfered school exercise book. Of course, we had to have a tipster's name just like the professionals in the national papers. There was Newsboy for the Mirror, Robin Goodfellow for the Mail and The Scout for the Express. These names are still in use today. Brian opted for 'The Judge', a name redolent of the forensic scrutiny of evidence. I plumped for 'The Magician' which conjured up images of 20/1 winners being pulled out of the hat. Patrick was 'Cool Hand Luke', later shortened to 'Cool Hand' which is not a bad nickname for a bespectacled sixteen-year-old to acquire.

This friendly competition intensified my interest in horse racing. My mum had The Mail delivered every day and was not fussed about me tearing out the racing pages before I left for school. We would sit in the sixth form common room reading the racing articles and studying the day's runners and riders before making our selections. I quickly built up a knowledge of top horses, trainers and jockeys, and also became familiar with the pattern of the racing year. Robin Goodfellow's reports would highlight the performances of horses who may end up being Champion Hurdle contenders or candidates for the Triumph Hurdle, and I soon picked up the idea of all roads leading to March's Cheltenham Festival. In the spring and summer, the focus was on the three-year-olds and the tussle for glory in the five Classics. In the autumn, attention turned to the two-year-olds who would be next year's Classic contenders.

What was really great about the Daily Mail – and I'm talking about horseracing here – was its publication of the number of days since a horse last ran. This meant that if I cut out the racing results from the newspaper and pasted them into another pilfered exercise book in date order, it was possible to look up a horse's last run. We had thus made, in true Blue Peter style, our own form book! A long way from today's interactive stuff I admit, but I remember how exciting it was to be able to trace back 19 days to some date in November 1974 and access the details of a particular horse's last run. This was cutting edge stuff.

The only thing we lacked was a racecourse in Sidcup. We soon fixed that. Sidcup Place is a small patch of green space that slopes gently down towards the river Cray and is located directly opposite the school. In those days, if you walked out of the school gate and crossed the road, you stepped onto the first fairway of a pitch and putt golf course. I say fairway, but as most of the holes were only 50 or 60 yards long, it was a reasonably wide strip of shorter cut grass. Ideal for a finishing straight.

The idea was to organise running races between those sixth-formers who were up for it and to make a book on which modest five-pence wagers could be placed. Despite our small size, we were quite a sporty school so the 'form' of nearly all of the boys was well known. We knew who the fast wingers were as well as the identity of the lumbering lock forwards. We also had summer term athletics form to go on. As is the case in most schools, it was blindingly obvious who the fastest boys in the year were, and it occurred to me that we needed a handicap system, or everyone would get bored seeing the same odds-on shots pulverising the opposition. We could have gone down the greyhound route and organised races restricted to runners of roughly the same speed, or we could align ourselves with horseracing and handicap by weight. The former was difficult as we didn't have a big enough pool of madmen to take part, so it had to be the latter which sounded much more fun and considerably more authentic. Who wants to be Mick The Miller or Scurlogue Champ when you can be Grundy, Bustino, Wollow or Brigadier Gerrard?

It didn't take us long to solve the problem of what to use as weights. Handicapping isn't an exact science, and nobody was concerned that they didn't know the precise weight to be carried by each runner. We typically had three or four participants in each contest and the fastest would be allocated the burden of carrying a Collins World Atlas and a copy of an A Level maths textbook. The second fastest boy might carry the atlas on its own while the bottom-weight would typically be allotted a copy of Anthony and Cleopatra, which was an A Level text in the 1970s. A racecard was published and pinned to the common room noticeboard detailing who was taking part, what books they were carrying, and the odds available for each runner. Brian and I ran the book with odds shortening and lengthening depending on where the money was going. It was all tuppenny ha'ppeny stuff and I don't know if anyone made any money out of the enterprise. But that wasn't the point.

What a sight these races were! They were held at lunchtime when sixth-formers had the privilege of leaving the site for an hour or so. Some viewed them from the safe distance of the second-floor landing area of the school building, its wide glass front looking directly down the finishing straight. Others preferred to be on hand to see the runners sweep into view from the bottom bend and cheer them home. I'm not sure what passers-by made of it all. Perhaps they just rolled their eyes at another example of the foolishness of youth.

Maybe they didn't. Perhaps they saw students filled with the zeal of learning, racing to their studies with enthusiasm and joy, carrying their precious books in each hand. Racing is all about perception and who knows what people are thinking when they watch a race.

They were happy days. Sixth form was great fun and most of the boys did well, growing in confidence, developing friendships and going on to work or further studies afterwards. St Mary's was a school for boys where several Marist (Society of Mary) priests taught and one of them, Father Greystone, was Head Teacher for quite some time. There have been plenty of depressing stories about harsh religious educational regimes and even abuse, but the priests who taught me were educated, enlightened and full of the humanity and compassion that the Gospels demanded of them. Who can forget the patience of Father 'Speedy' Norton, the maths teacher? Or the geniality of Father Murphy, who guided me through A level history? And I remember fondly the empathetic approach of Father Goonan, who taught RE and general studies, which touched on ethics and what it means to be human. When I married Jennie in 1990, we asked Father Murphy to officiate. He was delighted to oblige.

Funnily enough, despite our great sixth-form friendship built on a shared love of horseracing, Brian and I soon lost touch with each after university. He went to Durham to study Spanish while I tackled Modern History and Politics at Reading. I really can't recall either of us even attempting to make contact afterwards which seems strange to me now. But they were different times. As for Patrick, he stayed in the Sidcup area for a bit after his studies in Liverpool. We were even flat-mates for a while, renting in Blackfen and Barnehurst for a bit, sharing with a number of other local friends. When Patrick was relocated to Leeds with the Civil Service, we had already cemented a post-university friendship, a feature of which was, of course, our mutual love of horseracing.

23 December 2017

The latest video bulletin arrived from Newmarket. It showed Free Love cantering up Warren Hill. The accompanying message told us that we could identify her through the work rider's white Christmas jumper. Tom's update also confirmed that our filly had completed her half-speed work nicely. It was a lovely gift to receive and we returned Tom's seasonal best wishes. I wasn't sure whether Patrick had put a smartphone on his list when he wrote to Santa, but I was hoping it was as he was missing out on some great progress reports form Newmarket.

25 December 2017

We catered for 13 on Christmas Day. The full roll call was me, Jennie, my older brother Paul and our three children, Matthew, Celia and Joseph. Also present were Pete and Melanie and their two boys, Tom and George. Pete's mum, the sprightly Margaret was with us, as were Pete's sister Jane and her husband Jeff, who came up from South Wales to complete the party. I think we started alternating hosting Christmas day with Pete and Melanie just after my dad died, so for a dozen years or thereabouts both families were used to very full households on the 25th of December. We were four short of that record attendance of 17 held by the Smiths, but it made for a busy enough house.

These occasions are always great fun and usually end up with some absurd game once the pudding has been tackled and we have moved on to brandy and liqueurs. The children love it. I say children but the oldest, Matt and Tom, were 26 and 27 respectively that Christmas.

From a young age, the Linnett and Smith children were used to being in each other's company on special occasions and even on holidays. We've had many fabulous breaks in Pembrokeshire, Brittany, Normandy and Spain. Cricket and boules on the beach with barbecues back at the holiday cottage, that sort of thing. When in Normandy, a visit to Deauville races was usually on the agenda.

There were toasts to everybody's good health and toasts for absent friends. Some we would see in good time; some would never again be around the table. There may have been a toast to Free Love. I can't remember. I do remember being asked why we chose the name (nudge, nudge, wink, wink) and realised that I would need another digital recording for this one. How many times in the future, I wondered, would I be asked why we settled on Free Love? Would I become weary of explaining the witty allusion to the filly's sire and dam and be grateful for a button to press whenever quizzed about the matter? Only time would tell.

6 January 2018

The twelve days of Christmas came to an end, the decorations were packed away for another year, and the tree was taken to the local recycling centre. It was time to look to the future, so I came up with a plan for a get together of the owners. We hadn't visited the stables since October and now Free Love's work was beginning to be stepped up, it made sense to go and see her in action. Pete, Trevor and I could do Newmarket and back in a morning, so long as the Dartford Crossing was on form. For Patrick and Mick, York to Newmarket in a day was a bit more challenging, especially as they both tended to favour travelling by train. The idea was to have a day at the races somewhere near to Newmarket. We would then stay over for an evening and be in a position to get to Tom's yard early enough the following morning to see our filly do some work of the gallops.

Huntingdon was the ideal spot. The Sidney Banks Memorial Hurdle is one of the racecourse's feature races and it was due to be run on Thursday 8 February. I had been to this meeting in the past as it sometimes fell in the half-term break. Since retiring from full-time primary headship in April, I had plenty of time to devote to our horse project and was fairly flexible about when I could go racing. I still had a small educational commitment to fulfil, working one day a week supporting a new headteacher in a small primary school in Orpington. My regular day in school was Tuesday which could be moved if needed, but there were also governors' meetings to attend and with these I had very little room for manoeuvre once the dates had been agreed. Going racing on the 8th and visiting the stable the following day worked for me and I sent out an email to the others asking them what they thought of the plan, which also included a meal out in Huntingdon and a chance to agree racing colours. We could also have a look at our finances if we were enjoying ourselves too much and needed a change of mood.

Patrick and Mick got in touch quite promptly to say that they could make it. Patrick was only five months away from retiring and had scaled down to a four-day working week. Although Mick was retired, he had a substantial voluntary commitment to his church in York, but he was free on the proposed dates in February. That was the northern axis on board and I already had a thumbs up from Pete.

It was just Trevor to confirm, but I knew that his job might make it difficult for him to be away for the best part of two whole days. Trevor is a vicar, but this hasn't always been the case. He spent many years working for BT on the development side of their business and had a challenging job with plenty of responsibility. It must have been a brave decision for him to walk away from it. However, he saw this as a calling that had to be answered. He was already an ordained Anglican minister and had helped out for a number of years in his local church in Wilmington, mainly at weekends. With his four talented children either through university and working, or not far away from finishing their studies, Trevor took the plunge and applied for the post of vicar of a large church in Bexleyheath. He got it and with it came all the responsibilities of that office.

Trevor certainly wouldn't be able to come if he had an important church engagement during those two days in February. He also had commitments to two schools as a governor as well as other community roles he had picked up. But if it was at all possible, I was sure he'd be there. His interest in horse racing went back to his father who had shares in horses trained by Ted Long in Kent. One of them was quite a useful two-year-old, I believe. Trevor has fond memories of the family's involvement with racehorses and we both lamented the closure of Folkestone in 2012 where Trevor had spent many happy days in his youth.

Lovely Folkestone was Kent's last racecourse and I had fond memories of it as well. I wasn't a regular visitor though. The racing was usually moderate and I was always keener to go the big meetings elsewhere and watch class horses in action. I remember taking my oldest, Matthew, to a jump meeting in February half-term about 20 years ago, but my memory of a visit we made as a whole family on a sunny day in June 2007, is set clearly and indelibly in my mind.

It was Epsom Derby day. I don't know why we decided on a day-trip to Folkestone but went as a group and I think Pete and Melanie and all the children were with us. I remember watching Authorized bolt up in the Derby which was shown on the big screen located by the winning post. He scooted five lengths clear giving Frankie Dettori his first win in the Epsom Classic prompting the irrepressible Italian to celebrate in typically effervescent style.

I can't remember too much else about the racing that day, but I know for sure that Heart of the South had a runner. They also ran a competition where the prize was a free share in one of their racehorses. All you had to do was fill in an entry form, tear it out of the racecard and deposit it in a box near the paddock. This I dutifully did but without success. However, Heart of the South now had my contact details and emailed me soon afterwards consoling me on my bad luck while pointing out that failure in the competition needn't be a barrier to having a share in a horse!

The rest is history. They ran South Cape on that sunny June afternoon and he actually surprised everyone by winning a handicap by the narrowest of margins at a whopping 50/1. A couple of years later, after the disappointment of Clear Daylight, I had an opportunity to buy into the South Cape partnership. We had wins at Nottingham and Ascot from this game little gelding who at one point had a BHA rating of 100.

That may have been my last visit to Folkestone races, but it wasn't the last time I was at the racecourse. That happened on the way back from a headteachers' conference at the Hythe Imperial Hotel. The journey from Hythe to Dartford involved going right past the Westhanger turn-off which led to the racecourse. I couldn't resist. I didn't know what I'd find or even if I could gain access. What I found was sadness. The running rails were still up. The judge's box by the winning line still stood in lonely isolation looking forlornly down on the overgrown turf of the finishing straight. The stands were intact as were the buildings around the paddock which were in surprisingly good shape. The racecourse apparently hosted a two-day War and Peace Revival event in the summer. No doubt there would be jeeps, tanks, carrot cake, and plenty of volunteers in various uniforms. But there would be no more racing at Folkestone. The decision of the local council to develop the site had been made and I'll never again lean on the rail of its tree-lined, picturesque paddock watching thoroughbreds glide by with immaculately groomed coats shining in the warm summer sun.

I was sure that Trevor would definitely come to Huntingdon unless church commitments made it impossible. His racing pedigree ran deep. He was the last to confirm but it was a yes. It would be the first time that we had managed to get all five of us together since our visit to Tom's in October. I had already booked three twin rooms in the Premier Inn at Huntingdon on a fully flexible basis. Oliver Cromwell, here we come.

19 January 2018

The latest video from Wroughton House showed Free Love working upsides on the grass. It was slightly faster work and Tom described it as all quite straightforward. He confirmed that the filly was coming along well. It seemed to me that we were pretty much on course. Our trainer fully understood our position. We had bought a yearling with a precocious pedigree and, if possible, we wanted to be in action sooner rather than later. The well-being of Free Love obviously came first and if she needed a bit more time then so be it. However, Tom was working on the basis that we had an early season type on our hands and was preparing her for an April racecourse debut. It was still hard to believe that the little yearling we picked up at the sales only three months ago was perhaps only another three months away from being loaded into the starting stalls for her debut. So far so good, but I knew that there was plenty that could go wrong, and I needed to keep my feet on the ground and not let wild optimism get the better of me.

3 February 2018

It was time to start thinking seriously about racing colours. I had contacted a couple of suppliers who told me that once a design had been approved, the colours could be produced and delivered within a fortnight. However, I was warned not to cut it fine. Although

February was a fairly quiet period, things would get busier as the start of the flat turf season neared. I pinged round an email to the boys asking them to bring their ideas to Huntingdon. We could then make a final decision and have everything sorted out for the beginning of March.

Another great feature of the BHA website is its racing colours builder. Everyone should have a play with this. No special access is required. The colour builder shows the outline of a jockey with body, sleeves and cap, all in white. I knew that classy colours such as black body and sleeves with a white cap (Lord Derby), had long since been claimed and sure enough most of my attempts to secure something simple and eye-catching resulted in the 'colours unavailable' message popping up on the screen. It's probably why so many racing colours today look like a dog's breakfast as owners try to build combinations that haven't been used already. Mind you, there are strict rules on what your dog's breakfast can look like. Only specific colours and patterns are permitted. Hoops, stars, chevrons, checks, stripes, spots and even crosses of Lorraine are all allowed. However, it's hard luck if you want a tie-dye effect or something similar to Jackson Pollock's *Summertime: Number 9A*. As you can imagine, by the time you throw a handful of hoops, a bucket of stars, a bag of chevrons and the odd diablo or two at the blank jockey's outline, utilising several of the 18 available colours, you can end up with something pretty abstract looking anyway.

You can also end up with a big invoice. The more complicated the design, the more expensive it is to produce. It was therefore on the two counts of classiness and economy that I investigated simple colour schemes.

I was keen to incorporate orange and green. Me and Pete were founding fathers of a local football club, Old St Mary's FC. Between us we have made nearly 900 league and cup appearances and although our efforts on the pitch are limited these days to a couple of 'supervets' games each season, we are still very much involved with running the three teams we put out every Saturday. Pete is the Club Secretary while I'm the Chairman and Fixtures Secretary. We also have sons who now turn out for Old St Mary's. We both had the fabulous experience of playing in the same sides as our boys, as we dropped down to the third team in our old age and looked after Matt and Tom who were just starting their amateur football careers.

The club was created in 1986, loosely based around some former pupils of St Mary's school. We started off playing in the Old Boys League which was a huge competition for clubs whose membership was linked to a school. Hence, we played against the likes of Old Sedcopians (Chislehurst and Sidcup Grammar School), Clapham Old Xavierians (Clapham College) and so on. It was a league with great history and tradition, so it was hardly surprising that our efforts to join with a club name that paid homage to the brilliant 1986 Arc de Triomphe winner, Dancing Brave, was swiftly rejected. Instead of Old Dancing Braves we became Old St Mary's, although 'The Braves' has stuck as a nickname. You can still hear players and the odd older spectator shout 'Come on you Braves!' when encouragement is needed.

I bet we could have that name now. The Old Boys League merged with the Southern Olympian League and soon after the banks came on board. The competition was renamed the Amateur Football Combination and now a quick glance at the AFC website reveals that it is home to clubs with names like *Spaniards, Tilburg Regents* and *Rob Roy Reds*. By comparison *Dancing Braves* seems quite tame. I reckon you could even get approval for *Free Lovers FC* in these more enlightened and relaxed times.

The club colours haven't changed since we started up in September 1986 and have been defended against modernisers by the staunch traditionalists who have a vice-like grip on the running of the club (me and Pete). Why we chose tangerine tops and emerald green shorts in the first place is a story that belongs to Old St Mary's FC folklore.

The club was started by a group of friends – quite a few of them ex pupils, but by no means all – having summer evening kickabouts in Eltham Park, inspired by that year's eventful Mexico World Cup. As we moved into August, way beyond Maradona's 'Hand of God' goal and Argentina's ultimate triumph in the final, our Tuesday night football sessions at the park were still going strong. We all agreed that it would be a shame to let the football fizzle out as the evenings drew in and the light faded. Wouldn't it be great if we could organise an 11-a-side game against a real team? That's exactly what I did.

On Sunday 7 September 1986 a motley crew of eleven travelled to south-west London to play Deckers, a Sunday team for which one of my workmates at Wimbledon Greyhound Stadium played. (My brief involvement with greyhound racing is another story altogether). We didn't have a kit and decided that everyone should try to wear white. After all, most people can put their hands on a white top of some description. And white shorts are easy enough to get hold of. What a shambles! The team photo included a Cricklecock Cider tee shirt, an Argentinian top sported by Irishman Ray Gately (what else would he wear following *that* Maradona goal?!) and a melange of logos ranging from Puma to Man at C&A. And the result? A fashion own-goal and a resounding 10-0 loss on the pitch.

We were not to be deterred. At this time, Pete and Mel were married and living in Bristol. Pete hadn't been involved in the Eltham Park sessions but did play in the Deckers debacle and needed no persuading that a two-match tour of Bristol would be a great idea. All he needed to do was source opponents for a game on Saturday afternoon and another on Sunday morning – and work out how to put up eleven footballers and a number of girlfriends who thought a weekend in Bristol sounded like great fun.

This was serious stuff. A two-match tour of Bristol. We couldn't turn up in assorted white, grey, and sky-blue tops and a variety of white or pastel-coloured shorts. Even if we were rubbish, we could at least look the part. I took the executive decision to buy some kit and recoup my money by charging a £2 match fee whenever we played. If I kept to a strict budget of £100 maximum, I could get my money back over the course of four or five games. By now there was an appetite for more football, and I was sure this was a goer.

I made a visit to Gentry's in Welling. The shop no longer exists but for years it occupied large premises on the high street and was known as one of the best sports equipment suppliers in the area. The amount of stock held in this one privately owned shop was staggering, and I was hoping to pick up some old kit that they would be only too keen to get rid of.

I came straight to the point. What was the cheapest football kit that I could buy? The assistant disappeared into the back room and reappeared with a step ladder. He dragged down a battered brown cardboard box from a top shelf that was stuffed with neglected looking packages. He pulled out a lurid orange (officially described as tangerine) top and explained that I could have these for a bargain price as nobody else had shown much enthusiasm for the colour. And what about shorts? From another beaten-up box the assistant pulled out a pair of bright emerald green shorts. Ideal. Nobody wanted these either. The cheapest socks were white ones and by the time I added these plus a basic goalkeeper's top and kit bag, I was well within my £100 budget. This is how the iconic tangerine and green colours of Old St Mary's Football Club came into being, colours still in use more than 30 years later. Come on you Braves!

That's the explanation for the enthusiasm for featuring orange and green in our racing colours. My first attempts to go for something really classy – all orange with a plain green cap – predictably failed, but I was really surprised that the relatively straightforward orange body with green sleeves and cap combination, appeared to be available, so I reserved it. I gave my youngest son, Joseph, a go at it. Joe is the surprise package of the family. He is respectively, eleven and nine years younger than his brother Matt and sister Celia. He's been racing with me on many occasions and he knows his stuff. The horse that shaped his early experiences of racing was the mighty Frankel. I told him we were both lucky to be alive to see him in the flesh, Joe at Newbury's Greenham meeting and me again at York where Frankel sauntered away from a high-class field in his first attempt beyond a mile. Joe also worked with the St Mary's colour scheme and came up with orange and green hoops on the body with orange sleeves and cap. Again, I was surprised that these were available. Maybe I shouldn't have been if I remembered back to the battered brown box at Gentry's containing the tops that nobody wanted because of their garish colour. I reserved Joe's creation as well and called it a day. We had at least two options to consider when we met at Huntingdon, which was less than a week away.

5 Huntingdon

8 February 2018

It was bitterly cold at Huntingdon. I travelled with Pete but, due to work and family commitments, Trevor needed to go solo. The boys from the northern territories preferred the comfort of the train and, as we had two cars between the five of us, it would be no problem getting everyone from the course to the hotel and on to Newmarket the following morning. We all converged on the course at about midday and immediately found the sanctuary of a warm bar for a drink and a catch up.

Huntingdon is a charming country jumps track. I'm not sure about the chronology of recent developments, but it now boasts excellent bar and restaurant facilities catering for all tastes and pockets. I remember going to Fontwell decades ago, way before any improvements were made, and having the miserable sensation of not being able to find warmth anywhere on the racecourse. Things have improved immeasurably since, as has been the case with nearly all English racecourses. But they needed to raise their game. My first visit to the Newmarket Rowley course was probably in the late seventies or early eighties. What a disappointment. It was a dump! And that was the home of British racing. It's a pleasure to go there now and the same applies to the beautiful July Course just around the corner.

I was thankful for Huntingdon's modern and well-appointed facilities on a day which wasn't for leaning casually on the paddock rail watching the horses go by. Although we went outside to watch all the races – the viewing is excellent – we were quickly back in the bar as soon as the runners crossed the finishing line. It would have made sense to stay inside and view the action on one of the many screens perched high up in the bars, but I just can't bring myself to do that when I know that a few yards away the drama is unfolding in the flesh.

If we thought we had character by braving the elements, what about those men and women whose job it was to steer the horses round Huntingdon's tight bends, negotiating hurdles and fences at speed?

The excellent Adrian Heskin's day neatly summed up the vicissitudes of National Hunt racing. He had two rides. The first, Azzerti, was confidently ridden to victory in the feature handicap hurdle. So far so good. His remaining ride came half an hour later in a handicap chase. Minella For Me was disputing the lead as the field approached the first fence. The partnership glided over the obstacle only for the horse to stumble slightly on landing and slither to the ground, almost in slow motion. Fortunately, both horse and jockey were quickly up and clearly unharmed. Heskin looked aggrieved but philosophical as he walked slowly away from the scene of the mishap. Like all jockeys, he'd seen it all before. His partner galloped happily on, oblivious to the fact that he would be the only faller on the entire card. It's all about peaks and troughs and if you can't manage troughs as a trainer, jockey, breeder, owner or punter, then you're in the wrong game.

The main event, The Sidney Banks Memorial Hurdle, was won in decisive fashion by the highly promising Vinndication who retained his unbeaten record in doing so. It was four out of four for the handsome five-year-old gelding and our post-race chat inevitably focussed on his potential and what Cheltenham Festival race he might go for. He looked a top-class chaser in the making with an exciting future ahead of him. Who knows what peaks and troughs he will encounter in the years to come?

Pete and I had arrived early enough to check-in at the hotel and take a taxi to the racecourse. As Trevor was the last to get to Huntingdon, he drove directly to the course and was able to squeeze all five of us into his car after racing for the short journey back to the hotel.

I roomed with Trevor and the downtime before we went out in the evening was a good chance to catch up on what had been going on in our lives. I was interested to know if being a full-time Church of England vicar was what he had hoped it would be. Likewise, Trevor was keen to know how my part-time Executive Headteacher post was working out. We also had our usual discussion about church issues, ethics, and what was interesting in current affairs. When these subjects were exhausted, or we were exhausted by discussing them, we returned to horses, the subject that was the common thread uniting all five of us.

We managed to book a seven-seater cab to take us into town for the evening and headed for the river. Trevor and I had fond memories of The Old Bridge Hotel where we unexpectedly found ourselves one Christmas about five years ago. The second day of the big Kempton winter festival had been cancelled due to bad weather, but Huntingdon was still going ahead. As we were all dressed up with nowhere to go, we changed horses in mid-race and set off for Huntingdon instead. We had two cars of racegoers which included partners, children and friends and although there were sporadic flurries of light snow as we drove up the M25 and M11, both motorways were running well for a pleasant change.

We were within striking distance of the racecourse when it was announced on the radio that the meeting had been cancelled. I couldn't believe it. Out of curiosity I decided to complete the journey and fifteen minutes later I was driving into a sparsely populated course carpark. I got out and walked over to make a quick inspection of the track. I'm not sure what I intended to do. Approach the Clerk of the Course to tell him that he'd made a dreadful error and racing should proceed? The track itself looked fine but at the fence immediately beyond the winning post, snow had accumulated on its take-off side. I don't know how marginal the call was but if it was the same for most of the other fences and hurdles, then it would have been impossible to make jumping safe.

As we were in the middle of Cambridgeshire with nothing else planned, we decided to go for a drink and ended up in The Old Bridge Hotel. I'd often glanced to my right and seen the river and bridge at Huntingdon when making my way up the A14 to the north. It always struck me as an attractive location and, on this occasion, my instincts proved right.

The hotel was smart and comfortable. The main bar had a roaring open fire and a casual scattering of leather sofas and armchairs. We spent a very warm and chatty couple of hours in The Old Bridge before heading back home. All were agreed. We may have backed a loser in trying to save our day out at the races, but in The Old Bridge we had found a winner.

Five years on from my first visit, our seven-seater pulled up outside the same hotel. I'm long enough in the tooth to know that it's always dangerous to eulogise about an experience to others, then repeat it expecting it to be just as good. Trevor also remembered enjoying the hotel bar when we last visited following the abandonment of Huntingdon's Christmas fixture, but that was a while ago and things change.

I'm pleased to report that The Old Bridge has maintained its comfort and charm. The bar was as I remembered it, set a couple of steps down from the main level of the building, but other features were less familiar. I didn't recall the stylish reception area where smartly dressed couples were relaxing over shared bottles of wine.

The large restaurant to right of the bar didn't register either. The handpumps confirmed my memory of proper beer so we decided to stay for a drink at least. Within a very short period, we agreed to eat in the restaurant. On another occasion we may have opted for a curry and a pint but as we were going to discuss racing colours, finances and the detail of our partnership agreement, we decided to push the boat out. After all, in the context of committing £6,000 each to our horse project, £17.95 for crown of pheasant with a red wine jus didn't seem wildly indulgent.

Over the meal, our colours were agreed in seconds. Everyone liked Joe's effort, so orange with green hoops it was. The reserve on the colours still had a little time left to run and it would be a very quick job to sort this out when I got home.

Our partnership agreement was pretty straightforward as well. There are plenty of examples out there and some of us even had first-hand experience of signing up to one. I played around with a few templates and came up with something that fitted onto a single side of A4. I'm not a fan of lengthy documents and my old Deputy Head, Jayne, teased me in the presentation she delivered on my retirement day, that I was forever telling people that I wasn't interested unless whatever was being proposed could be expressed on a single side of A4 paper. Funny how you can go through life not recognising your own idiosyncrasies and mannerisms that others see only too clearly.

This was a single side of A4, with only eight numbered points. Succinct. Some of those points stated the obvious. We needed to confirm the names of the partners and the fact that we were equal 20% stakeholders. Another point confirmed that all prize money would be held in a Weatherbys bank account and shared out equally at the end of the project. Any shortfalls in cash would need to be met equally as well. The cornerstone of the agreement was that the partnership would run until the end of October 2018 when the filly

71

would go to the Tattersalls horses in training sale, unless **all** members agreed on another course of action. To bail out early or carry on beyond the agreed one-year period of ownership required everyone's approval.

After the meal we went into the centre of town in search of good pubs and good beer. Patrick had noted that The Falcon was renowned for its wide selection of real ales, so we headed there first. True enough, there was an impressive row of handpumps on the bar, but it was a quiet and cold Thursday in February and the pumps comfortably outnumbered the customers. We read inside that the pub was used as a recruiting station by Oliver Cromwell for the New Model Army. This surprised me as I always took the Horrible Histories line that Olly wasn't jolly, and felt sure that he wouldn't been seen dead in a pub. He wouldn't have done much business had he tried his luck on this particular night. Five blokes all either rushing towards 60 or already beyond that milestone, and a couple of loud locals. A dog, I think, as well. Not much to go to war with.

We decided to move on and finished the evening in the Samuel Pepys, a pleasantly modernised pub opposite St Mary's Church. It obviously got the thumbs up from members of the choir who piled in after their weekly practice. We chatted the evening away over a couple of pints. The talk wasn't all about Free Love but some of the conversation reflected the growing optimism in the camp. Tomorrow we would hear it from the horse's mouth.

9 February 2018
The weather forecast was spot on. My wife, Jennie, often derides my unalterable faith in the accuracy of the Met Office app, and the family joke is that we can be standing in the pouring rain, but I'll tell everyone that, according to the Met Office, it's dry, or at least it should be. On this occasion it was raining, just as predicted. It was a

drab, overcast morning. The fine drizzle that greeted us as we clambered into the cars was due to linger for another hour but would hopefully clear by the time we were standing on Newmarket Heath.

Tom had said that he could arrange for Free Love to work with the first lot at 8.15am or the second lot which would go out about an hour later. We opted for the later slot and we were on the road just after eight. The journey was a bit of a slog. It was rush hour on the A14, but we arrived in good time and as if by the magic of the Met Office app, the rain eased, and the sky brightened.

Tom and Jackie gave us their usual warm welcome and after a quick hot drink we made our way to the gallops. Although Tom's yard is walking distance from the bottom of Warren Hill, it's easier and safer to hop in a car and park somewhere near the top. During the short walk from the cars to the railed gallops, we walked past Michael Bell with whom Tom exchanged early morning pleasantries. John Gosden was there, as was the urbane and smiling Roger Varian who greeted us with a friendly hello from the top of his docile hack.

The visit was a reminder of how tight-knit the Newmarket racing community must be. I think there are over 70 trainers operating out of the town, all using the extensive facilities on the heath. We were just a tiny part of it, the optimistic owners of a small, bay filly whose 10,000 guineas purchase price was small change for considerably wealthier owners who have some of the very best thoroughbreds in the world stabled in this small patch of Suffolk.

Free Love did two nice canters during which Tom told us that he'd like to think that our filly would be his first two-year-old runner of the season. She had done everything asked of her to date in a very straightforward way and was proving to be an amenable learner. Back in the office, Tom's assessment of how things were going prompted a short conversation about where and when we might make our debut. Tom didn't want to rule out an all-weather track as he felt these surfaces were safe introductions for young horses. But I was already dreaming of the two-year-old race for fillies at the Newmarket Craven meeting in mid-April.

I knew the race well and had already looked up past runnings. They were a bit hit and miss in terms of field size and quality. In 2017 there were only eight runners and the winner, Formidable Kitt, now had a current BHA rating of 75 and looked to be on a downward curve. The runner-up, Take Shelter, was also on 75 and looking similarly in decline. No world beaters then, and I couldn't help but dream of a debut at the home of British racing. Imagine that? At Newmarket for the Craven meeting – as an owner!

Tom and Jackie gently threw a couple of buckets of cold water over my romanticised vision of Free Love's debut. Jackie mentioned that she was pretty sure that Rizeena had made her debut in that race. She was right. My subsequent research revealed that Rizeena built on the promise of her fifth-place finish on debut at Newmarket with wins in the Queen Mary Stakes at Royal Ascot in June and, a year later, in the group one Coronation Stakes again at the royal meeting. Over the years there have obviously been one or two useful sorts introduced via that particular Newmarket race and Jackie clearly thought the opposition might be too hot for our little filly.

Tom wasn't keen on Newmarket for other reasons. He explained that our filly was slightly offset on her off-fore and pointed this out as she walked around the yard after exercise. It was hard for me to say with certainty that I could see this but thought it best to just nod in agreement. Basically, it meant that one of Free Love's legs wasn't as perfectly straight as it should be, which is a common enough feature of plenty of racehorses, apparently. In some cases, the fault can be pronounced enough to put off would-be purchasers, (my mind went back to the yearling on our Tattersalls shortlist that Jackie ruled out) but this clearly wasn't the case with our girl. Tom's view was that a track like Newmarket with its dip and little undulations wasn't an ideal surface for a young horse with this minor conformation defect. I think his take on this was influenced by an injury sustained at Newmarket by one of his horses with a similar physique. To be on the safe side, he advised that we stick to flat tracks, so the likes of Newmarket, Brighton, Ripon and Goodwood were off the agenda for the time-being.

Despite my dreams of a Craven meeting debut vanishing into the damp February air, it was a really positive visit. I told Jackie that we had finalised colours and instructed the local suppliers to make them up and deliver them to the yard. Everything else appeared to be under control and Tom suggested meeting up for lunch towards the end of March when we could sit down and discuss specific races in which Free Love could make her racecourse debut. There was also the photo-shoot after exercise. Our little filly stood quiet as a lamb while we patted her and generally fussed over her while gathering more snaps for the album.

Before going our separate ways, we went to Nancy's tea room, which is just a few minutes' walk from the stables. Nancy's is a delightful place selling various loose-leaf teas served in a wide range of unmatching but stylish vintage teapots and crockery. For the hungry there is breakfast, for the indulgent home-made cakes. When finished, we persuaded one of the waitresses to take a group picture of the five of us seated on the sofa and chairs set into the bay window which was etched with 'Nancy's' in large, swirling script. It was hardly an image of the wild men of racing. You could almost smell the Earl Grey when looking at it, but we didn't care. We had got ourselves a racehorse and the wild times lay tantalisingly near at hand.

17 February 2018

Around a week after Huntingdon, Tom's latest video update showed Free Love doing a nice sharp canter, upsides a stablemate. He explained that our filly's workload was gradually being increased and as a result she was now on full feed. We had pencilled in the final pre-season stable visit for 23 March. It couldn't come soon enough.

The wild men of racing posing in Nancy's tea room, Newmarket.

6 False Dawn

Since the last video bulletin from Newmarket, there had been the distraction of the Cheltenham Festival but even the excitement of the Prestbury Park annual showcase couldn't stop the weeks from dragging. At last the day of the stable visit arrived.

We arranged to meet at Tom's at 9.30am which was a bit of an ask for Patrick and Mick coming down from York, but they made it. We were on the heath again watching our filly canter up the hill. It was another raw, blustery day. Apart from confirmation of Free Love's wellbeing, the canter didn't provide any new, vital information. That was to come later.

Tom told us that as horses stepped up their work and were put through their faster paces, trainers needed to find out if the animals in their care had sufficient raw pace to be racehorses. His rule of thumb was that, at their fastest, thoroughbreds should be able to run a furlong inside twelve seconds. That equates to approximately 40 miles per hour. If they haven't got the raw speed, then forget it. But having the raw speed on its own is not enough. It needs to be sustained and can only be done if the horse possesses the willingness to keep going, to keep putting in the effort even when tired and finding it tough.

Tom confirmed that Free Love had shown the requisite speed, but it was Jackie's understated comment that really made me prick up my ears.

'She's not a dud. I can tell you that,' was her almost throwaway remark.

High praise indeed! Everyone involved with horses knows that many of them will never make it. Maybe they haven't got quite enough natural speed. Maybe they don't want to exert themselves too much – the clever ones perhaps? I think experienced horsemen and horsewomen know a dud when they sit on one and as far as Jackie was concerned, Free Love was no dud.

That was an uplifting piece of analysis. All along I thought the odds were in our favour. In conversation with anyone foolish enough to show an interest in my horse project, I kept repeating, almost like a mantra, that the full-brother and sister both won races, and both won as two-year- olds, so statistically our filly…I got fed up of saying it in the end, but I really believed it. The percentages **were** in our favour and it wasn't unrealistic to expect Free Love to follow in the family tradition and win a race or two. That's all we wanted - a genuine racehorse, perhaps rated 75 or thereabouts, who would give the five of us plenty of fun and some experiences to remember for the rest of our lives. After all, although the odds of winning a race were marginally in our favour, the odds of ever being able to do this again were stacked against us.

The less uplifting piece of news concerned our eligibility for the Newbury Super Sprint and auction races in general. It transpired that it was our **ineligibility** that was the issue. Tom had telephoned me about a week earlier to ask how I felt about entering Free Love for the big sales races for which she qualified. We agreed the Newmarket race over six furlongs in October wasn't realistic but Newbury's shorter test over five furlongs, which is run in July, would be worth a crack. After all, Tom's Declarationoflove had picked up over £52K in prize money when finishing second to Bengali Boys in the 2017 renewal of the race. At the time Declarationoflove had a modest BHA rating of 79.

Jackie had gone ahead with the Newbury entry and was surprised to learn that Free Love didn't qualify. The race is for horses bought at public auction up to a certain price. Expensively purchased horses aren't eligible and the weights allocated are directly linked to sale prices. The less an owner spends on buying their horse, the less weight the horse will carry in the race. Crucially, prices paid through private sales don't count. For the Newbury race, with its huge prize money fund, and for tiny class 6 auction races devised to help small owners of cheap horses compete against each other without bumping into a multi-million-pound Godolphin purchase, Free Love was not allowed entry as she was a 'private sale'.

I could see the sense is trying to stop sharp practice. Nobody wants to see a low weight allocated to an expensive yearling in a valuable sales race like the Super Sprint as a result of somebody holding a piece of paper confirming that in a private (bogus) sale the horse was sold for buttons. If I had the resources, I suppose I could breed a potentially expensive foal and 'sell' it to my wife privately for 1,000 guineas (I'm generous to a fault) and produce a bill of sale as proof of the transaction. The horse would then be eligible for auction races big and small and would carry a featherweight in them because of the pitifully low sale price. I understood all of that. It just seemed so unfair in our particular case.

Despite this apparent setback, we had left Newmarket in really good spirits. Tom persuaded us that a debut on the tight but safe all-weather surface of Chelmsford might be a good starting point, but this was almost certainly ruled out now as it was an auction race. There were alternatives at Leicester and Nottingham to consider.

We chatted about our options over lunch in the Palace House Museum restaurant. There we were, in the centre of Newmarket, relaxing in part of a former stable complex originally built by Charles II and now home of the National Horseracing Museum, talking with our trainer about the plans we had for our filly. Bruce Hobbs was the last trainer to operate out of Palace House, sending out 48 group race winners in his time. Some of them resonated with my youth. Tromos,

Tyrnavos and Tumbledownwind were just a few that achieved racecourse glory for Captain Hobbs and his owners. These horses would have occupied some of the boxes just a few paces across the courtyard outside the restaurant. No harm in dreaming, I thought.

Tom and Jackie left us to it as we continued chatting about race options over coffee. I said I'd ask for clarification about the auction race eligibility business when I got home and report back to everyone. All smiles, we shook hands and went our separate ways, hopeful that we would be reunited on a racecourse within the next three weeks.

24 March 2017

The journey home was straightforward and on reaching Dartford, Pete, Trevor and I made a quick visit to the Malt Shovel to mull things over and see if we could get hold of anyone at the BHA who could tell us if it was just Newbury's Super Sprint that we were barred from or was it all auction races. I was pretty sure I knew what the answer would be and the following day I emailed everyone with the news:

Gents,

Let's get the bad news out of the way first.

The Dartford contingent had a pint on our return from Tom's and again looked at race options. This prompted me to make a quick call to BHA/Weatherbys to check our eligibility for auction races. As feared, we don't qualify for such races which means that Chelmsford next month is not an option.

The person I spoke to was pretty clear about it and when I checked the BHA's glossary of race types, I found that the definition talked about only 'under the hammer' prices counting and NOT private sale prices.

I know it all sounds unfair as we paid the 5% commission to Tattersalls (it's a rule that private sales can't be used to avoid paying the auctioneers) and the sale is shown in their Book 3 list on the Tattersalls website. However, like a number of other transactions, the letters 'P.S.' are shown in brackets after the price indicating that this was a private sale and the 10,000 guineas price tag was not arrived at 'under the hammer'.

I can't see a way round this. It's consistent with the line given by Weatherbys about the Super Sprint conditions of entry and by the BHA person I spoke to on the telephone about the matter.

We are OK for median auction races (entry determined by sire's progeny sales prices) and I attach a list of new possible targets. Maybe Leicester on the 13th?

And the good news? We are still eligible for the Molecomb, Flying Childers and Prix L'Abbaye!

Regards, Tony

We had just been ruled out from a whole tier of races designed for smaller owners like us. I wrote what I felt was a reasonable and balanced letter to the BHA about the matter, having agreed with the others that I would do so. Tom told me that the issue had been raised by the National Trainers Federation. He observed that he ran a two-year-old in a maiden auction race last season who had been subject to a private sale. I didn't hold out too much hope that my representations would change the thinking of the BHA, but I felt I had to give it a go. This is how it went:

Dear Sir or Madam,

RE Eligibility for Auction Races

I am writing to express my belief that the current stipulations for eligibility for auction races are unfair and in need of review.

Subsequent to purchasing a yearling at the Tattersalls Book 3 Sales in October 2017, we discovered that our filly (Lot 1383 Equiano ex Peace And Love, registered racing name FREE LOVE) would not be eligible for auction races as our transaction was deemed to be a 'private sale'. I am all for a fair and transparent system that prevents dishonest practice, and nobody wants the purchase prices attached to dubious private sales to give owners an unfair weight advantage when entering horses in auction races. However, I would dispute that our purchase price constitutes anything other than a bona fide auction figure for the following reasons:

- The filly was led out unsold at 11,000 guineas
- We made an immediate offer to the vendor of 10,000 guineas which was accepted, and 5% commission was promptly paid to Tattersalls

Our transaction was transparent, made in good faith, very publicly recorded and subject to all the rules of the sale including the payment of full commission to the auctioneers. Barring our filly from auction races therefore seems both unreasonable and unfair.

Free Love is the first racehorse we have bought. The North South Syndicate is made up of five enthusiasts on a strict budget. Naturally we are disappointed at not being able to enter the Weatherbys Super Sprint (this is when the problem first came to our attention) but being ruled out from a whole tier of races, suitable for small owners, because of a poorly phrased rule is frustrating to say the least.

Perhaps a clear agreement is needed between the BHA and those running specified sales about what constitutes a private sale and what can be reasonably deemed a purchase price that is derived from the process of horses physically going through the sales ring.

I await your comments with interest.

Yours faithfully, Anthony Linnett, Syndicator/Owner, The North South Syndicate

The reply from the BHA was perfunctory and didn't tell me anything I hadn't already stated in my letter to them. It was short and sweet:

Dear Tony,

Our Racing department has responded as follows:

Private sales are excluded from auction race eligibility because they are open to manipulation. It would be easy for a vendor to lead a yearling through the ring unsold, having set an unrealistic reserve price, only to register a private sale for a

very low price and thus gain an unfair advantage in auction races. By selling on the open market, whether bought in or sold, the price arrived at is a much fairer reflection of the value of that horse and much less open to manipulation. This rule has always been in place, as far as I am aware.
Regards, BHA

I can't pretend that this wasn't a significant setback. We knew when we bought Free Love that she wasn't part of the Plus 10 initiative. Plus 10 is an industry-funded scheme for British and Irish owners and breeders. Basically, the breeder pays a £350 registration fee for the foal and the owner pays a similar amount when purchasing the yearling. Further payments must be made by specified deadlines for eligibility to be maintained. If the horse goes on to win one of the designated Plus 10 races, a £10,000 bonus is shared between the owner and breeder. We knew that Free Love hadn't been registered for the scheme when she was walking around the sales ring, and my subsequent enquiries confirmed that we couldn't pay the registration fees retrospectively. We knew all that. It didn't bar us from running in Plus 10 races. It just meant we wouldn't get a bonus if we won one of them.

Being barred from auction races was a much bigger blow. Some of these races can be quite weak with entry restricted to horses who cost less than 25,000 guineas at public auction. It struck me that the best way forward was to get in our three qualifying runs as quickly as possible so that we could run in nursery handicaps which started in July.

28 March 2018

The dream was becoming more and more real. Tom's message and video clip received this morning took things to another level. Sent as usual via WhatsApp, his short bulletin was upbeat:

Good morning all. Here is Free Love (middle, red cap) working over five furlongs this morning under Josephine Gordon. She does it nicely, she is straight and ready to run. Josephine liked her, I hope everyone is well and it was great to see you all last week. Best, Tom.

I watched the 28 second video several times. This was a genuine piece of fast work. The three horses involved weren't hanging around and our filly seemed to travel well throughout, unfazed by having company on either side. I assumed that one of the other horses was Gypsy Spirit, a cheap 6,000 guineas buy from the Doncaster yearling sales. Gypsy Spirit's relatively new sire, Gregorian, was a tough seven-furlong specialist and I remember Tom mentioning last week that she and Free Love were his two most forward youngsters. If Josie Gordon liked our girl that was good enough for me. Josie's career had really taken off in the last two seasons and she was regularly used by Hugo Palmer who had established himself in a relatively short time as a leading Newmarket trainer. Our racecourse debut was surely only a fortnight or so away.

29 March 2018

It was my 60th birthday. The spring term had finished and there was a fortnight or so when I could forget about my part-time school job. It was part-time and looking likely to be short-lived. I had been working on the school budget for the 2018/19 year and beyond, as one of my tasks was to sort out the staffing structure and put the school on a sustainable financial footing for the future. Things had been going well in terms of supporting the new head and working with the governors, but it was becoming increasingly clear that the budget wouldn't sustain a part-time Executive Headteacher's salary unless it was subsidised by the Academy Trust. That was unlikely to happen, so I had already started the process of writing myself out of plans for the school's future. I was the turkey who voted for Christmas.

Mind you, it was just as well that it was a part-time job, as the Free Love project was consuming a fair bit of my energy. It was something I didn't begrudge though. Far from it. It was great to be in a position where I could afford to spend less time working and more time pursuing my interests and other voluntary commitments.

Jennie had asked me what I wanted to do for my birthday, and I assured her that I didn't want a big party. I'd already expressed an interest in taking (forcing) the whole family to go to the Good Friday performance of The Messiah at the Royal Albert Hall, which is a sublime experience. We had gone on our own several years ago, and it would be a much-appreciated gift if all the children came as well on this occasion to have some culture inflicted upon them. That's what I wanted to do.

The other thing I wanted to do was visit the Turner Contemporary in Margate to see an exhibition of art curated by local people designed to visually interpret T S Eliot's epic poem *The Waste Land*.

I know, I know. Isn't this all very pretentiously high-brow for a horseracing obsessive? Not really. Like many of my contemporaries, classical music wasn't an integral part of family life - although I did have six months scratching away at the violin in primary school, giving up before somebody killed me. I just found that my musical tastes broadened as I got older. I now have a fairly eclectic set of playlists and will happily listen to anything from Iggy Pop to The London Philharmonic Orchestra on Spotify. In any event, *The Messiah* is a deeply moving and spiritual creation entirely fitting for a Good Friday, a day when I should be in church at 3pm for the solemn service that all good Roman Catholics attend. If I couldn't be in church, at least I could assuage my catholic guilt by attending a live performance graced with the soaring beauty of the *Hallelujah Chorus*.

As for *The Waste Land*, I studied the poem as well as *Prufrock and Other Observations* for A Level. When these books of poetry weren't being used for handicapping purposes, I read them with real pleasure. I'm sure my old English teacher, Mr McMahon, would be pleased to know that his teaching inspired enthusiasm, and not just competency in exams.

I've always liked poetry and there's something fabulous about being able to recite by heart a bit of prose or even whole poems. I have many favourites. *The Sunlight on the Garden* (MacNeice) *He Wishes For The Cloths Of Heaven* (WB Yates) and *To His Love* (Shakespeare) represent an uplifting, if rather middle of the road, handful taken straight from *The Nation's 100 Favourite Poems* book. I don't know of any famous poems about horseracing, and I won't be attempting to put that right. I've long accepted that I haven't the ability to write poetry. I just scribble down the occasional puerile limerick when the mood takes me, and they're hard enough to get right.

We set off for Margate quite early and arrived at the Turner Contemporary in time for breakfast. It was just me and Jennie. I felt very at ease with my age and very comfortable with my company.

The exhibition was fabulous. What a project this had been! A large group of locals, from incredibly disparate backgrounds, had come together to study and discuss *The Waste Land* before deciding what art they would curate for the exhibition. Some came with great knowledge of Eliot's work and of art, others came with nothing. They were advised by the staff at the centre who obviously helped to acquire various pictures and objects. Other pieces were created specifically for the exhibition. Some worked better than others but if ever there was a case of the whole being greater than the sum of its parts, this was it.

It was really appropriate that the project was conceived in Margate. The town has gone through some rough times, but a better, brighter future hopefully lies ahead. It was a quite fashionable and well-regarded place when T S Eliot was convalescing there during a period of depression. *On Margate Sands, I can connect nothing with nothing,* is a fragment from *The Waste Land,* believed to make direct reference to Eliot's frame of mind during his stay at the coastal town. In some respects, the poem had come home.

We had a great day which included a drink on the way home in a cosy, out of the way village pub. It had all gone so well until an unwanted birthday gift turned up in the early evening. Tom's message arrived at 6.13pm.

Good evening all. Sadly, Free Love has sore shins at stables this evening. It's very common and not the end of the world, it just means she will need a quiet couple of weeks. Therefore, touch wood, we will be on the track at the end of April/early May. Her jacket isn't quite there yet and theoretically she isn't two either so it's just nature's way of telling us to go a bit steady. Hopefully it also means once she gets racing it won't happen again. I hope you all have a good Easter. Tom

I reflected that things had been going almost too well. I also felt a twinge of guilt. We gave Tom the brief of buying a precocious type who would be able to make her debut right at the start of the flat season. Financial constraints played a big part in this strategy. We didn't have enough money to be patient. Had our desire to move things on quickly been responsible for this setback? Tom was right. Free Love was still a baby. Although sharing the same 1 January official 'birthday' with all thoroughbreds, she wouldn't actually turn two until 25 April.

Perhaps we just didn't have enough money to be proper owners, was my gloomy thought. After all, the welfare of the horse must come first and if we put that at risk because of our tight budget, maybe we shouldn't be in the game. But we all had fallen in love with our filly. There was no doubt about that, and we knew we had to leave everything in Tom's hands, who had shown in our dealings with him that he was a real horseman who cared deeply for the animals in his care.

Throughout the whole project, I was the one who kept repeating the dire warnings about what could go wrong, telling the others that we might not even see a racecourse for our £6k (while all the time secretly hoping for spectacular success). At this stage there wasn't that much of our money left. We were waiting for a VAT reimbursement which was part of the Tattersalls sponsorship scheme. This was taking an age to go through. Since last October we had spent around £13k to purchase Free Love and complete all the necessary registrations. We had shelled out a similar amount in training fees. It was a sobering experience to look at our Weatherby's online racing account statement and observe the sharp decline from £30k in October to around £5k just six months later.

It was a setback. Hopefully that's all it was. I couldn't do anything about it other than get back into the BHA website and look up races at the back end of April and early May that might be suitable for us. I could spend hours doing that.

30 March 2018

My children endured The Messiah. That's perhaps a bit unfair. Joe, who had turned sixteen three weeks earlier, found the experience the most challenging but even he had to admit that there was something special about being at a live performance with an orchestra, outstanding lead singers and a choir which ran into hundreds. He conceded that it was a fabulous sound. He just felt that shortening the experience by about an hour would have made it even more fabulous. He even gave advice on which bits could be ditched.

I don't think I was distracted by thoughts of Free Love during the performance, but I can't guarantee that she didn't cross my mind. There were definitely thoughts of horseracing though. Over a drink in the large theatre bar behind the stalls, Matt, Celia and Joe presented me with my 60th birthday present. It couldn't have been better. Two top tickets to the Prix de l'Arc de Triomphe with Eurostar travel thrown in. How brilliant was that!

I had been to the Arc once before. In 1983 I booked an all-in package deal with Patrick which involved an arduous return coach journey from Victoria. There was no overnight stay in Paris, and we slept in snatches on the coach and ferry. I remember leaving Longchamp immediately after the last race on Sunday and stepping off the coach in London just after dawn on Monday, blinking in the autumn sunshine, rubbing sleep out of my eyes. All Along won the race, ridden by the late Walter Swinburn, whose angelic features earned him 'the choirboy' as his nickname. I can't remember much else about the trip, but I was there, and I was going to be there again 35 years later. And yes, the thought did cross my mind. Two-year-olds are allowed to run in the group one sprint on Arc day, the Prix l'Abbaye, and in 1978 one of them actually won it.

12 April 2018

Much sooner than anticipated, Tom was in touch with encouraging news. His message took me by surprise. I wasn't expecting to hear anything for a while and when it came, I was bracing myself for urgings of patience. I had prepared myself for a much longer period of inactivity, but we learned that Free Love had started cantering on Tuesday and her summer coat was beginning to come through. Her shins seemed fine and Tom was hoping that this little setback was behind us. It was hard to infer from the bulletin when Free Love was likely to make her racecourse debut, but it sounded like weeks rather than months.

13 April 2018

The good news kept coming. Tom provided a short video clip of Free Love doing a steady canter up Warren Hill. She was on her own and it was all very sedate stuff. However, the accompanying message was full of optimism. *She looks great and I am pleased with her,* was our trainer's observation. It was very much a case of 'game on' again.

20 April 2018

Morning all. Free Love worked on Wednesday. It was straightforward, but she did it fine. She'll need one more bit of work before she runs. I hope everyone has a good weekend. All the best, Tom.

We bombarded Tom with comments and queries following this update. Everyone was anxious to know our likely target so that they could clear the decks in order to be there. A novice race for fillies at Kempton on 1 May was looking to be the one. That was on Tuesday, the day I set aside to work in school, but I had a fair amount of flexibility about when I did my support. It was also one of Kempton's twilight meetings and our race was scheduled for 6.15pm, so I didn't anticipate a problem getting there even if I had to do a bit of work first. Initial entries had to be made by noon on the Wednesday before, which meant we were only five days away from seeing the name 'Free Love' appear in a racecard on the Racing Post website. Her pedigree analysis, auction price (best not start on that one again), racing colours and ownership details would all be there. At that point, it would begin to feel real.

23 April 2018

I'd been following all of Tom's runners, willing them to perform well, but Gypsy Spirit's debut at Windsor caught me by surprise. I had been out and about and casually switched on the television to watch a bit of the *At The Races* coverage of the evening meeting at Windsor. I noticed that the next race was a two-year-old contest and I was pleased to catch it as I was already making careful notes of the results of juvenile races, sizing up what might be Free Love's opposition in the near future.

I remembered that Tom said his Gregorian filly would be making an early debut, but I didn't press him about where and when. By sheer coincidence, I had tuned into *At The Races* minutes before Gypsy Spirit was about to show everyone what she could do.

She was nibbled at in the market and the early 25/1 had gone. She was a 14/1 shot as she approached the starting stalls and seemed to go in without too much bother. I imagined how I would feel if Free Love got upset and refused to load, leaving an impatient starter to withdraw her before sending the other runners on their way. That would be unbearable. There were no such nightmares for Gypsy Spirit, but it had the makings of a bad dream as she dwelt slightly when the starting stalls opened and immediately had Josie Gordon pushing away in an effort to keep her mount in touch.

The filly responded to Josie's forceful but rhythmic urgings and as the field swung right and straightened up for the final three furlongs, Gypsy Spirit moved up strongly towards the outside. Just before the final furlong, Josie gave her young charge a flick of the whip. One more tap, accompanied by more vigorous pushing, ensured that Tom's first two-year-old runner of the season crossed the line with a neck to spare, giving the strong impression that there was more to come.

You could read it whichever way you wanted. Tom's small string had made an excellent start to 2018 and this was more evidence of the good health and general wellbeing of the horses stabled at Wroughton House. I was pretty sure Gypsy Spirit had worked with Free Love recently. Not completely sure though, and even if she was one of the three horses charging up the Newmarket gallops in Tom's video, all you could tell was that Free Love *appeared* to work well with her. Beyond that it was hard to say. I hadn't quizzed Tom about the identity of the three horses, what approximate weights they carried, and which one had worked best. I was just fairly sure that we had done a nice piece of work alongside Gypsy Spirit with Josephine Gordon riding our filly.

It was encouraging. I could at least say that. I didn't back her, but I think Mick had a couple of quid each-way and one of the guys I play golf with backed her thinking that Gypsy Spirit was our filly! Despite my attempts to bore him to death with bulletins about progress and my theories about Free Love's pedigree, the name of our horse evaded this golfer, but he knew she was trained by Tom Clover, so he backed Gypsy Spirit just in case. He even got a bit of 25/1.

25 April 2018

Afternoon all. Here is Free Love doing her last bit of work before she hopefully runs at Kempton on Tuesday. She seems to be moving nicely and is enthusiastic in her work. Will see how many entries there are in the next hour or so.
Best regards, Tom.

It was a fitting way for Free Love to celebrate her second birthday and hours later there we were on the Racing Post website shown as an entry for the *100% Profit Boost At 32Redsport.com EBF Fillies' Novice Stakes (Plus 10 Race) 5 Furlongs, Class 5.*

A click on Free Love's name took you to her profile. Obviously, there was no racing record but everything else was there. Below the little picture of the orange and green colours, was confirmation that this horse was owned by the North South Syndicate. Brendan Boyle was shown as the breeder and the pedigree, going back to grandparents (another click on these would take you back further into the family tree) was accompanied by a brief analysis: *10,000gns yearling; fifth foal; sister to winners Lydias Place (5f inc at 2; RPR 90) and Lawless Louis (5f-6f/ GB 2yo/ Qatar; 81), half-sister to 7f-1m AW winner Dimitar (76); dam 5f 2yo winner (74), out of useful 1m2f winner.* No mention of a private sale then, but we'd done that subject to death.

29 April 2018

Declarations had to be made by 10am and, as expected, Free Love appeared in the list of confirmed runners which was released soon after the deadline. The race looked hot enough. The likely favourite was Kodinar, a Kodiac filly who was a half-sister to seven winners and trained at Newmarket by the absurdly successful William Haggas. Kodinar had finished fourth on her debut at Ripon and looked sure to improve for the experience. Others to fear included Mick Channon's Chyna who had run with promise when a close fifth on debut in the Newmarket fillies race that Tom was keen for us to avoid. The unraced On The Stage, a 20,000 guineas Swiss Spirt debutant trained by Ed Walker, was strong in the market suggesting she had been showing up well on the gallops at home.

There were ten runners in all, and, on initial analysis, my head said that a first four finish would be a really encouraging start. We could finish sixth and still have made a creditable debut. As for my heart, well that was something completely different, at odds with logic and experience.

30 April 2018

Tom gave his thoughts about the race via email. He was concerned about the wide draw – we were in stall 8 – and he said that he would tell Josephine to tuck in and give Free Love a nice introduction, trying to finish as close as possible without having a hard race. After all, we wanted our filly to have a positive first racecourse experience. It was more important that she learned from it and her enthusiasm for racing wasn't tarnished by an unhappy first day at the races.

Tom felt that the race was pretty competitive, and he singled out Kodinar as the most likely winner. He commented on the good form of Mick Channon's two-year-olds which made Chyna a danger, along with a number of nicely bred fillies from fairly big yards who were making their racecourse debuts.

I busied myself with the business of allocating badges to owners and guests via the relatively new *Racepass* online system. Patrick had been dealt a decent hand at work. He was in the London area for a couple of days and he would make his own way to the track. He was sure he could get there in time. Mick was initially unsure as a day return from York to Kempton by train would be a long and tortuous journey but when I offered to put him up for the evening, that made things much more manageable. Pete was always on board, as was his wife Melanie. Jennie would be able to meet me at the racecourse coming directly from Dulwich where she works part-time for a local charity. Which just left Trevor. Unfortunately, our full-house was thwarted by his evening commitment for the Diocese at West Malling which made it impossible for him to catch the race and get to his appointment in Kent afterwards.

It was a shame that we all couldn't be there for Free Love's first outing, but we accepted that if we gave Kempton a swerve and waited until everyone could be present, our filly might not see a racecourse until October. My youngest, Joseph, would also be an absentee. Poor old Joe. He was about take eleven GCSEs which involved around 25 separate exams either side of the May half-term. I had talked through a sensible revision strategy with him that involved around two hours a day and the coverage of all subjects twice throughout each week. In other words, little and often, leaving time to keep his hobbies and interests going. Joe decided to stick with the programme and give Kempton a miss. I didn't put any pressure on him either way, but I knew he'd have loved to come. There would be another time, I assured him.

7 Kempton Debut

1 May 2018

It had been a relatively calm and untroubled voyage of just under seven months from the Tattersalls Book 3 Sale to Kempton Park racecourse. I suppose it hadn't been a very long time to wait, but my daily anticipation of this moment made it feel that my first visit to Tom's yard was an event from the distant past.

It was a lovely, bright evening. Although the floodlights would be switched on for later races, they wouldn't be needed to help Free Love see which way to go. Because of the time of year, and weather that hinted at the arrival of summer, Kempton had attracted a fair crowd. Fair by the standards of these rather quiet twilight meetings, that is. It was nothing like the crowds that flock to Windsor on Monday nights. Go there in the height of summer and it looks as if most of London's young office workers have downed tools early and jumped on a train to the leafy surroundings of that charming riverside course.

Kempton is more functional and for that reason it can hold a big crowd. For the same reason, it's easy for a small attendance to get lost in its vast grandstands, but it wasn't too bad a show at all on this first day of May.

We were there in plenty of time and had a brief chat with Tom and Jackie before they went to saddle a two-year-old making its debut in the auction race. Tom confirmed that our filly was well, and he was hopeful of her running a 'nice race'. The draw and the track were concerns. Most five-furlong races are run on straight tracks, but at Kempton the sprint course starts almost on top of a bend and horses are quickly on the turn as soon as they leave the stalls. A slow start is something to avoid at all costs.

I congratulated Tom on Gypsy Spirit's winning debut at Windsor and in conversation about how the two fillies might compare, Jackie remarked that Gypsy Spirit was perhaps 'more streetwise' than our girl. Only time would tell what that meant.

Tom's Rajy ran well enough in the auction race showing promising speed on the outside before getting tired and fading into ninth place in a field of eleven. She was only beaten about eight lengths and I asked myself if I would be disappointed if Free Love made a similar debut half an hour later. The honest answer was yes. Realistically, that's exactly what she could run like and it would be something to build on in the future. But I was hoping for a fair bit more.

We had good news leading up to the race. Kodinar had been withdrawn, as had a newcomer who wasn't fancied very much in the betting. The field was now down to eight and, as the first four won prize money and would go into the winners' enclosure after the race, I had visions of a bright start to Free Love's racing career. In truth, my thoughts were grander and more expansive than securing a bit part in the winners' enclosure. What if she pinged the stalls and travelled strongly on the heels of the leaders? What if Josie Gordon sat motionless as the field swung into the straight and all around her were pushing, shoving and rowing away? What if the merest shake of the reins was enough for Free Love to bound clear and coast home for a facile and decisive victory? Now was the time to dream.

I needed to calm down. Such heady thoughts make the disappointments all the more crushing. It was time to go to the pre-parade ring to see our filly being saddled. At Kempton this area is a fair distance away from the main paddock and it's also where the horses who finish out of the frame congregate, their unsmiling jockeys waiting for morose owners to join them for stony-faced post mortems. I hoped we wouldn't be meeting Josie there after the race and my mind travelled back to November 2007 and my brief discussion with Dane O'Neil after Clear Daylight's frustrating handicap debut. That memory served as a timely reality check.

Our filly was turned out in great shape by Tom. She still looked a bit on the small side, but compact and in proportion. She's never going to be big, I thought. I knew that she'd strengthen-up over time but also knew that she would remain a relatively small racehorse.

It was in the main ring that Free Love showed her first signs of inexperience. Quite understandably, two-years-olds often find the whole business of parading with other horses, while being watched close-up by crowds of people, bewildering and off-putting. One or two of them were getting a bit fractious and this seemed to affect our filly who was becoming a little restless herself. As I was observing this, Josephine Gordon came into the paddock wearing our orange and green colours. After some quick introductions Josie confirmed what she hoped to do in the race. In her words, it was Free Love's 'first day at school' and she would do her level best to get the filly as close as she could while making sure her initial racecourse experience was a positive one.

The horses were soon filing out of the paddock and onto the course. Free Love continued to be a bit on her toes but once down at the start, the pictures on the big screen showed that she was reasonably calm. She was one of the last to enter the stalls but did so without fuss, much to my relief.

I didn't know whether I felt excited or sick. The betting offered few clues and was an irrelevant sideshow as far as I was concerned. We were steady in the market at around 10/1 but it was all guesswork. Yes, Tom had scored with his first juvenile runner of the season. Yes, the stable was in good form. Yes, Free Love's pedigree was full of speed and winning two-year-old relatives. Yes, we had been working nicely at home doing everything that could be reasonably expected.

Did I know any more than that? Not at all. They're the facts I told to anyone who wanted to listen before saying that they must make up their own minds about parting with their hard-earned cash. I had a tenner each-way, but only because I was obeying the unwritten law requiring owners to back their own horses at all times, regardless of the scale of the task faced.

I had my binoculars trained on the orange jacket in stall eight. Hardly anybody uses binoculars at racecourses these days and owning a pair is a badge of age. The big screens bring the action to you. You'll see a handful of more senior racegoers using them and, like me, they would feel naked on the course without them. In our defence, it allows us to focus on what we want to look at which is not always what you see on the screen.

I was looking exclusively at Free Love and Josephine Gordon as the track commentator announced, 'They're off and racing.' The big screen showed a head-on view which confirmed that our filly had made a sluggish start but the side-on view given by my binoculars painted a more alarming picture. Not only was the start slow, Free Love gave no indication that she understood she was now required to gallop a bit quicker and catch up with the others. From being left by a couple of lengths, the gap between her and the rest of the field quickly grew to five lengths, then ten, then fifteen.

'As they swing into the straight with two furlongs left to run, the one who's completely outpaced is Free Love,' was the commentator's final mention of our filly.

I knew I wasn't dreaming. I knew this was real. It was a living nightmare unfolding before my eyes, but I couldn't take it in. It was as if I didn't fully understand what was going on. How could everyone be so wrong? Another newcomer, On The Stage, was pulled out from behind the leaders with a furlong left to run. She quickened smartly and put the race to bed in the blink of an eye. I had time for quite a few more blinks before Free Love passed the wining post in eighth and last place 16 lengths (yes, sixteen) behind the seventh horse and beaten 28 lengths in total.

I can't remember exchanging a word with the others during the race or immediately afterwards for that matter. Somewhere deep in the pit of my body, I felt a pang of dread and guilt. I had a host of half-formed questions swirling in my head as I marched grim-faced to meet Free Love and Josie. Tom came over and said something about being really sorry and how embarrassing it was for him as a trainer. I didn't take it all in.

When I arrived at the designated area, tucked behind the pre-parade ring and miles away from the winners' enclosure, Josie had already dismounted, and the filly was being walked round by a stable-hand. Free Love appeared fine. Josephine didn't. She looked shell-shocked.

'I can't understand that. I came here thinking I must be in the first three. I rode her work against Gypsy Spirit, and we walked all over her. I don't know. Maybe six furlongs, maybe soft ground…'

Josie's voice trailed away as she stared at Free Love in disbelief. This was not the de-brief we had anticipated. On Kempton Sands, we could connect nothing with nothing.

2 May 2018

We stayed on at Kempton for a few more races before going our separate ways. The car journey home was pretty subdued. Mick stayed in my daughter's old room and over breakfast we tried to make sense of last night's catastrophe. There was nothing physically wrong with our filly. By mid-morning Tom had provided an update: *Good morning all. Free Love ate up well last night, she has trotted up okay this morning and seems bright in herself. Once again, apologies for yesterday, hopefully we can put a line through it and look for a much better performance next time.*

I'll be in touch soon to see how she is out at exercise and with dates for a next run. All the best, Tom

If there was nothing amiss with her health, there were only two possible explanations for last night's dismal showing. It could be a matter of total greenness, with everything happening far too quickly for our little filly, who acted like a startled rabbit in the headlights. Josie had felt that Free Love wasn't letting herself down properly and if that wasn't due to a physical problem then it could only be something going on between her ears. Which brought us on to the second possibility. Perhaps she just didn't like it and won't ever like it. Maybe it was a case of won't rather than can't.

But that didn't make sense. 'The Equiano filly', as Free Love was rather literally known at Tom's before she was officially named, had done everything asked of her with the minimum of fuss. I had seen her on the gallops with my own eyes. Maybe that was it. Maybe our baby, and she was still a baby, had pulled the wool over everybody's eyes with her placid and compliant temperament, giving the impression that she would take her racecourse debut in her stride. Jackie's prescient comment about Gypsy Spirit being more 'streetwise' came to mind.

I had a cup of coffee in Dartford town centre with Mick before seeing him off at the train station. We didn't restrict our conversation to horses, which is just as well, as we were going round in circles with that one. I became even more aware of how involved Mick had become with his local church in York and it was fascinating to hear about all the very practical voluntary work undertaken, helping others both within the church community, and through growing outreach work in the town. By comparison, me taking a busman's holiday once in a while to sort out activities for young children during the family mass on Sunday seemed like small beer.

17 May 2018

Things had gone a bit quiet, so it was good to receive a WhatsApp message from Tom. The video clip showed Free Love doing a fast piece of work upsides two other horses. She was in the middle and appeared to be breezing along. There was no lack of enthusiasm here. Tom said that he was really pleased with her. I had already started looking at possible races. We all agreed that we wouldn't press the panic button just yet, and would stick to five furlongs, preferably on a nice level turf track. There was a race for fillies at the end of the month at Nottingham which was on Tom's radar. With my 'interfering owner' hat on, I suggested that this looked ideal for us. It was also ideal for Patrick and Mick who could get there in under two hours by car.

18 May 2018

Hot on the heels of yesterday's bulletin, Trevor sent a photo update from the stable which he visited on his way to see his daughter in Norwich. Tom was only too happy to accommodate an impromptu drop-in if he could. The pictures matched Trevor's observation that Free Love's coat was gleaming, and she looked in great shape. During the visit Tom confirmed that it remained all systems go for Nottingham. It was also all systems go for Tom and Jackie's wedding which was to take place the following day.

19 May 2018

Tom and Jackie couldn't have picked a better day to take their vows. It was an absolute belter. They were sharing centre stage with another couple being married on that scorching day in May. It was the Lockinge meeting at Newbury and I persuaded Jennie that a visit to the races, courtesy of the ROA's free tickets scheme, where we could sip Prosecco while watching coverage of the royal wedding on the big screen, would be a perfect way to spend this idyllic late spring afternoon.

We didn't give Harry and Meghan our undivided attention, but it was a pleasant enough backdrop to the day. We sat on one of the benches on the large lawn in front of the relatively new and stylish Berkshire stand to take in the scenes from Windsor. To my left, in the distance, stood the familiar line of poplar trees past which I'd seen Zeta's Son, Sea Pigeon and other heroes of bygone times glide by. They were still and statuesque, barely a leaf stirring in the warm, breathless air. I'd only need one glance at that line of trees to know I was at Newbury.

There was a decent crowd, an encouraging feature of which was the strong showing of relatively young racegoers. That particular group was bolstered by my eldest son, Matthew, who was with a large crowd of 'the lads' to celebrate his 27th birthday which was only three days away. We hadn't told Matt we were going and took him by surprise when we ambushed him in the Crafty Filly bar behind the Berkshire stand. He was delighted to see us, really. We had no intention of cramping his style and left him to his entourage after a quick drink. There were plenty of familiar faces. Many were school friends – Matt is part of an unusually large group of very close pals who have socialised from sixth form onwards. There were Lancaster University chums as well. Pete's eldest, Tom, was present, and he and Matt provided a bit of expert insight for many of the other boys who were there just to dress up and have a day out. Seeing your children in good company is something that gives great pleasure to all parents. Mind you, I can only guess at what their girlfriends make of it all. It's like being married to the mob.

Rhododendron won the big race for Aidan O'Brien under a power-packed ride from Ryan Moore. The same Ryan Moore who had won on South Cape for Heart of the South at Nottingham in

103

October 2010 when Trevor and I had a share in the horse. I always thought that it was both strange and fabulous that a jockey could win the Arc de Triomphe for a wealthy, perhaps royal owner in Paris on Sunday and a few days later ride for an assorted group of Clapham omnibus characters in a low-grade race at some unglamorous provincial racecourse.

The horse that made the biggest impression at Newbury was the three-year-old filly Sea Of Class who got off the mark in spectacular style at the second time of asking. I consoled myself with the knowledge that Sea Of Class was green on her debut and this was a significant step forward. On the other hand, she had been runner-up at Newmarket on her first attempt, not last on the sand at Kempton beaten over 28 lengths. I decided it wasn't a very good comparison and it didn't provide much comfort on the journey home.

28 May 2018

We were declared for the Nottingham race. So were 16 others. It wasn't quite the gentle second run we were looking for. Of the 17 two-year-olds, a handful had some racecourse experience, but most would be making their debuts. Among them were several with decent looking pedigrees. Heartwarming, a half-sister to the Royal Ascot Queen Mary Stakes winner caught the eye, as did Richard Fahey's 180,000 guineas purchase, Kodyanna. It looked a red-hot heat and even at this stage I thought we'd do well to finish in the first ten. The finishing position wasn't that important, though. What we wanted was to see Free Love race with purpose for at least some of the contest. In other words, we desperately needed to avoid another Kempton.

29 May 2018

I was at the computer sorting out the badge allocation for our race and had made a mental note to watch Gypsy Spirit's second run which was at Lingfield that afternoon. She was tackling six furlongs for the first time and as the only previous winner, she was required to give weight away to all her rivals. She went down fighting but had no answer to Octave's finishing kick in the short home straight. Mark Johnson's well-backed Dawn Approach filly justified odds-on favouritism by overhauling another newcomer close home. Gypsy Spirit could only plug on at the same pace to finish a respectable third. It was a solid enough run under a penalty and a return to the minimum trip looked a likely next move. At this stage, Free Love's galloping companion was clearly ahead of the game.

8 Nottingham

30 May 2018

The southern part of the North South Syndicate set off from Dartford. Trevor offered to drive and picked up me and Pete just before nine. We thought we could make it for noon and with our race scheduled for 2.20pm, that would give us plenty of time to relax, have something eat and study a bit of form.

I had taken a good look at our race the day before, but its complexion altered significantly after prolonged and heavy overnight rain. Tom's initial concerns about quickish ground were swept away under 13mm of water. The going description of 'good to firm' had been changed to 'soft' within 24 hours.

When we arrived at the course we were greeted by pools of water in the carpark, evidence that it must have really hammered down in the early hours. We had no idea how Free Love would cope with the conditions but there seemed to be little point in withdrawing her as she needed the racecourse experience. She would take her chance and we were sure that Josephine Gordon, who we were lucky enough to book again, would look after our filly and not give her an unduly hard race if she got tired in what would be very testing conditions for young horses.

Patrick couldn't make it because of work commitments but Mick trained it down from York and we met him in the owners and trainers' bar. The room was a decent size and we had no trouble in finding a table. The omens were good. We had been warmly greeted by all the staff on duty and after a wholesome lunch we were already positively inclined towards the racecourse. I hadn't been since South Cape won the first of his two Nottingham races just under ten years ago and thought that the owners and trainers' facility looked new or perhaps it had been upgraded since my last visit. It was a good start to the day.

The signs continued to be positive. A trickle of non-runners had become a steady flow with horses pulled out on account of the going. A total of 18 were withdrawn at the meeting including five in our race. I was pleased to see that the non-runners included Heartwarming. Sabai Sabai, a 260,000 guineas Shamardal filly trained by Ralph Becket, was another absentee. She wouldn't be missed. Tom even withdrew his own Hunni from the fillies race later on. She had raced on heavy ground first time out and hated it so much that it was decided not to risk her again.

I had no idea whether our filly would love or loathe the ground. She might be indifferent to it for all I knew. Whatever she felt about it, so long as she showed even a glimpse of what she had been doing on the gallops, it would be a step in the right direction.

We went to the parade ring where Free Love was led in looking very well and on good terms with herself. Minutes later, Josie walked over to our little group. It was all smiles. Everyone agreed that we should put a line through Kempton and start from here. We chatted briefly about the draw which had not been particularly kind to us. We were in stall 15 which meant we had just one outside us to the right. It would have been better, perhaps, if we had been dealt a middle berth which would have guaranteed that Free Love was racing in company right from the start.

Soft ground, an outside draw, coming into a hot race on the back of a debacle of a debut. Things felt a little less positive than they did when I was tucking into my lunch while looking at the growing list of non-runners displayed on the television screens in the bar. As Free Love left the paddock to canter down to the start, I walked towards the stands and had my obligatory fiver each-way at 50/1.

As at Kempton, my binoculars only had lenses for one horse. Our girl was the second to go into the stalls. She went in calmly, but it took an eternity to load the other eleven and all the time I was staring at Free Love praying that she wouldn't get restless or upset. Worse still, she had enough time to go to sleep. At last, the final horse consented to enter his stall. The handler scampered to the side, the yellow flag fell, and they were off.

Free Love was out and racing! After the first hundred yards it was obvious that this was a different horse to the one we saw freeze in the stage lights at Kempton. She Can Boogie broke fast to our right, which was a big help, as the main group raced a little bit away from us in the centre of the course. With She Can Boogie to keep Free Love company, we were no more than a couple of lengths off the pace at halfway, lying in about sixth position. At the two-furlong pole Josie gave her mount two flicks of the stick but when it was obvious that her partner would not be troubling the judge, down went the whip and our jockey rode out with just hands and heels in the final furlong. Free Love got understandably tired and faded into eighth place behind the Mick Channon newcomer, Gospel. Kodyanna was a promising third and by the time our filly crossed the line, she was 12½ lengths adrift of the winner.

That was much more like it. Free Love had shown some speed. She couldn't sustain the effort in the holding ground or at that stage of her career, but it was the step in the right direction that we were all hoping for.

At Nottingham, horses finishing outside the first four are brought back into the pre-parade ring which is adjacent to the main paddock. By the time we got there, Josie had already jumped off Free Love who was being offered a well-deserved drink of water. We were all smiles. I joked with Tom that he should have more owners like us – eighth place and we're celebrating! Josie was pleased with the filly's much improved effort as well. She said that Free Love got tired towards the end in ground that she probably didn't like. But that was perfectly understandable as this was effectively her debut. Her Kempton experience hardly amounted to being in a race. Josie's parting comment was more upbeat on this occasion. She watched Free love being led round but this time there was no shellshock or bewilderment. Josie simply told us that we should have a lot of fun with our filly.

The fun had already started. We all gathered round Free Love and took more photos which we quickly shared via the WhatsApp group. When was Patrick going to get that smartphone? I wasn't sure what I was going to do with all these photos. I already had hundreds and that was after just two runs. Perhaps it would be a project for me when I was fully retired, and my weary limbs didn't want to go swimming or play golf anymore. I would print them all out and buy a huge leather-bound album and sit in the shade of the willow tree in my back garden, sifting through the memories and creating the definitive pictorial record of Free Love's racing career. I would call it *The Free Love Story* and even include cuttings from all the racecards that I save in numerous drawers around the house. Yes, that's what I'd do one day. It's the type of thing we all promise ourselves that we'll get around to, but in the meantime, I'd just keep taking pictures.

31 May 2018

Morning all. Free Love ate up well and is sound this morning. There are a couple of options for her third run. June 13th at Yarmouth and 18th at Windsor. There is the 10th at Nottingham but I fear this could come a little too soon. Great to see most of you yesterday and will be in touch. All the best, Tom.

Yarmouth sounded good to me. It was one of 18 English racecourses that I'd yet to visit. That's quite a lot for somebody who's had such an enduring interest in horse racing, but I've rarely gone to courses just for collecting purposes. Normally it's because I wanted to be there for a big race. For that reason, Newmarket, Cheltenham, York, Sandown and other top venues were ticked off the list early. Going locally for a nice day or evening out meant that the likes of Lingfield, Brighton and sadly missed Folkestone were covered. Opportunistic strikes when on holiday accounted for Ludlow, Wincanton, Ripon and other rural courses. And ownership through penny-shares took me to Leicester, Bath and Nottingham to name but a few. But Redcar? I'd have to go some to get Redcar into the schedule. And what about Cartmel? It's miles away and only has a handful of meetings each year.

A bit like the photo album project, when the dust has settled, I'll have to make a point of completing the set. But it's not on the bucket list. If push came to shove, I could receive the last rites and feel no need to express remorse about failing to make it to Redcar, Cartmel or any one of the other tracks that I haven't managed to visit yet. In truth, I'm not really the bucket list type anyway. But if I did have one, it would only have two words on it. Free Love.

2 June 2018

On the day that Masar won the Epsom Derby pocketing £850,000 for his wealthy owners, I received the May invoice from Jackie and knew that we couldn't afford to pay it. We were still waiting for our first VAT reimbursement, which would be around £4,000 as it included VAT paid on the purchase price for Free Love. We had a fighting fund of £30,000 to start with and it was nearly all gone. It highlighted the expense of racehorse ownership, particularly those associated with buying a yearling. If we had gone to the Tattersalls sale in July for horses in training, we could have bought an experienced 70 rated handicapper for about 10,000 guineas who could have been running for us a month later. You pay for your dreams though. Between October, when a yearling is bought, and its debut 6-9 months later, anything is possible. The dream is nurtured, protected from harm until the first racecourse appearances are made. As a long-standing racing pal of mine once observed, owning horses is such a fabulously enjoyable experience – until they start running.

We needed to pay a bit more for our pleasure and I asked the boys to top up the account to the tune of £800 each. That would get us through to when the VAT cavalry came charging to the rescue. It was like the old racing joke about the student who liked to dabble on the horses. His letter home to his long-suffering parents simply stated, 'System working well. Please send more money.'

Right from the start, we knew we would run out of cash by around July if we hadn't won a penny in prize money, so the calculations were about right. We all topped up the account and kept our fingers crossed for two things – somebody at HMRC getting their uncrossed finger out, and Free Love getting her hooves into gear sooner rather than later.

9 June 2018

Tom decided to send Gypsy Spirit to Beverley for the Class 2 Hilary Needler Trophy, a conditions race for fillies with a decent first prize of over £20,000. I knew about this race as it was seen as a possible stepping-stone for the Queen Mary Stakes at Royal Ascot which took place two weeks later. Over the years I had taken an interest in its winners. Easton Angel was a very smart recent victor who went on to finish runner-up to the brilliantly fast Acupulco at Royal Ascot. I was familiar with the Beverley contest for other reasons as I had trawled through the BHA website looking at all the five-furlong races that Free Love could go for. Sometimes I applied filters to my search on the basis that we would need to target modest affairs with prize money not exceeding, say, £8,000. On other occasions I played the 'what if' game and looked at all the fancy early season options for two-year-old fillies. The Hilary Needler Trophy was one of them.

Gypsy Spirit was relatively unfancied at 25/1 but she comfortably outran those odds. Always prominent on the inside, she had no answer as our friend Kodyanna swept by at the furlong pole, but she kept on determinedly for third place beaten only a couple of lengths. I could only imagine how ecstatic the members of the Gypsy Spirit Partnership must have been with their 6,000 guineas bargain buy. Was I envious? Of course I was.

That's more like it! A smiling Mick Corringham after Free Love's improved effort at Nottingham.

9 Yarmouth

11 June 2018

Tom decided that Yarmouth was our best bet and we were declared to run with eight others. The race was a Class 4 novice event for colts, fillies and geldings with reasonable prize money. Reasonable by British standards, that is. Although only nine would go to post, the field certainly wasn't lacking in quality. There were a number of expensive purchases from the Newmarket breeze-up sale held at the Craven meeting in April. I've never been to this type of event but have seen video clips of young horses sprinting solo over two or three furlongs for the benefit of prospective purchasers. The pedigree, physical look, and time clocked by the youngster, are all considered before the bidding starts.

In the case of two runners, the bidding must have taken a while to stop. Deputise represented the powerful William Haggas yard and the owners had to go to 110,000 guineas to secure this son of Kodiac. That was a nice profit for whoever paid 70,000 guineas for him as a yearling. But that was nothing compared to Motogally. His owner, Hamdam Al Maktoum, went to 200,000 guineas to add this Swiss Spirit colt to his bulging bloodstock portfolio. Not a bad return for whoever snapped up the colt for a mere 25,000 guineas as a yearling.

Of those with racecourse experience, Phoenix Star caught my eye. He had finished last of seven on his only run to date, but he blew the start before getting into contention at halfway. He weakened approaching the final furlong and wasn't given a hard time by his rider. After watching the Racing Post video replay a couple of times, I felt that he had shaped much better than his finishing position suggested. Silvestre De Sousa's booking caught the eye as well. Artair had won earlier in the season on soft ground but was well beaten at

113

Sandown when upped in class. Penalised for his win, he now had to give weight away to all on what was a much quicker surface.

I thought we had an outside chance of making the first four. We knew that Kempton was an aberration and if Free Love built on the promise she showed at Nottingham, perhaps improving for better ground, then we might trouble the judge. I couldn't put it any stronger than that. It would be a fiver each-way for me again.

13 June 2018

It was another hot day. The warm spell showed no sign of breaking and the official going description at Yarmouth remained good to firm which was only achieved by prudent watering of the track. It was Mick's turn to miss out. He had a church commitment and couldn't get there but Patrick, who with Mick must be keeping the national railway lines running, intended to come, his train arriving in plenty of time for our race. Trevor would go solo and take the opportunity meet up with his daughter in Norwich afterwards.

Pete and I left early making sure we arrived an hour before the first race, something I do more and more these days. I've had too many experiences of sprinting onto the course as the horses are filing out of the paddock, leaving me feeling rushed and unprepared.

Before we left, I had my ritualistic each-way bet but chose to ignore my racing pal's advice about the level of the stake. I've known Kieran since university days. He didn't go to Reading but bumped into a Reading contemporary, Tim, on a bus destined for Haydock Park. They started chatting about the racing and found out that they had something else in common. They were both at law school having completed their degrees the previous academic year.

I've kept in touch with Tim and Kieran for the best part of four decades. Sometimes we get lazy and won't see each other for a few years, but the Ebor meeting at York in August is where we usually reassemble and have a chance to catch up. Racing is the glue that holds us together.

While Tim has steadfastly and sensibly declined to buy into a horse, Kieran has dabbled in racecourse ownership and proved to be a successful dabbler as well. He's been a junior partner in a number of horses trained at Newmarket by Chris Wall, some of which have been no good at all. But he did have one really good one, the type that comes around once in a lifetime and only in the lifetime of the lucky. He had a quarter share in Donna Viola, who improved through the handicap ranks to win a Group 3 race at the Curragh. Her final run before being sold to race in the States was at Longchamp on Arc day, where she got up close home to land the 1996 running of the Group 2 Prix de l'Opera. What a sensational experience that must have been, one never to forget nor likely to be repeated.

Kieran's staking advice for Yarmouth was bold but not foolhardy. He was the one who coined the quip about ownership being such great fun in the months and weeks leading up to when the racing begins. After that it can often be a series of crushing disappointments as all hope sinks like a stricken ship, dragged down by the weighty realisation of the horse's limitations. On this occasion, Kieran was being positive. We were at the crossroads, he reasoned. Now was the chance to get it all back. He advised £100 each-way at 100/1. We wouldn't see that price ever again if Free Love was any good. Seize the day!

I told Pete about Kieran's advice as we drove through the flat terrain either side of the A47 east of Norwich. I had stuck with my fiver each-way and had taken 100/1 before we left Dartford. Being more circumspect, Pete declined to disclose if he had already backed Free Love and to what stake. I felt I was on pretty safe ground thinking that it wasn't £100 each-way, though.

It was my first visit to this seaside course and on arrival I was struck by its sense of space. The expansive flat track sat beneath a big, cloudless sky. Shirt-sleeved racegoers eating ice creams stood chatting in the sun. It was a school day, but the crowd wasn't lacking in youth as there were a fair number of couples with pre-school toddlers and babes in buggies. The atmosphere was relaxed as a small part of England's population took in the races during their holiday on the coast. The sense of tradition was upheld by the beautifully preserved wooden judge's box which looked down on the finishing line from the far side of the track. Its brilliant white body was supported by four tall, green stilts which elevated the viewing platform some twenty feet above ground level. It looked as if it could be a listed building and was a throwback to an era before photo-finish technology was introduced, and the outcomes of tight finishes were decided by eagle-eyed officials looking down from their lofty perches.

We made our way to the owners and trainers' restaurant which was an attractive summer marquee in front of the permanent building which housed the bar. I opened the racecard to see what was being said about Free Love. It confirmed that Bhangra was a non-runner making the race a field of eight. The *Timeform* comment for our filly read: *Twice-race maiden. 8th of 12 in maiden at Nottingham (5f, soft, 50/1). Others much preferred.* It was hard to argue with that assessment, but we knew – ok, hoped - Free Love was better than that.

Tom was soon on the scene and he was in a pretty upbeat mood. He was confident that our filly had improved since Nottingham and was hopeful of a 'nice run.' 'Nice' could mean anything though. I thought Phoenix Star had run 'nicely' on debut despite finishing last, 13 lengths behind the winner. (It encouraged me to have a disloyal couple of quid on him to win at 12/1 as a 'saver', and an even smaller forecast bet on him to beat us). Free Love had already run twice, so last of eight today beaten 13 lengths or more wouldn't be 'nice' in my books. However, sixth or seventh and only beaten half a dozen lengths? I'd probably take that. We just wanted to see more progress. We wanted our girl to race with enthusiasm, look like she was enjoying this newish game, and indicate that she could become a real racehorse.

Josephine Gordon wasn't at Yarmouth and Tom had secured Jack Mitchell to take the ride. Jack was having a good season and had ridden plenty of winners for Roger Varian in what appeared to be the role of second jockey behind Andrea Atzeni. It meant that Jack got to sit on his fair share of classy animals and was often entrusted with looking after some of the stable's young horses during the early part of their racing careers. It looked to be a good booking for our filly, who was still on a learning curve.

Jack entered the paddock and was all smiles. He shook hands and, unprompted, told us that Josephine had spoken well of our filly. I wasn't expecting that. Not only had Jack taken the trouble to get in touch with Josie about Free Love, he had also received positive feedback from her. Tom talked to Jack about trying to get a lead in the hope that Free Love would be able to finish off her race. He was expecting her to come on a fair bit for the run in the Nottingham mud. Seconds later, Tom was giving Jack a leg-up which meant another photo opportunity before we headed to the stands.

Everyone behaved themselves at the start and, unlike Nottingham, Free Love didn't have long to wait before the rest of the field was loaded and the starter was ready to dispatch the eight runners. The flag fell, the stalls flew open and both Deputised and Motogally missed the break and were soon three or four lengths adrift. But I wasn't taking too much notice of them. Artair was leading and just in behind was Free Love who was trying to pull Jack's arms out of their sockets. She was taking a fierce hold and refused to settle in what looked like a slowly run race by sprint standards. On the one hand I knew that pulling so hard meant burning up energy that would be needed at the business end of the race. On the other hand, I was pleased to see her racing so keenly.

As the field approached the two-furlong pole, Free Love was tucked in behind Artair who was bringing the main group of six down the middle of the track. Suddenly, Silvestre De Sousa switched Phoenix Star to the stands rail, leaving Free Love to make her effort widest of all. Then something magical happened. As the runners approached the final furlong Free Love began to overhaul Artair and for a split-second I swear she was in front. A split-second later, Phoenix Star's strong run up the stands rail swept him into the lead and at the line it was a one-two for those who elected to come up the rail with Free Love winning the race in the middle to finish third overall.

It was a four-man pandemonium! We'd been screaming on our filly inside the final furlong and, as she flashed over the line, we raced down the steps in a state of frenzy.

'Was that yours?' enquired a stable hand as we rushed by him

'No! No! The third!' I yelled. I didn't stop to catch what must have been a bemused look on his face.

We arrived at the winners' enclosure ahead of Jack and Free Love. There was no disguising our excitement, pleasure and pride. We had a racehorse! We had a proper racehorse! Boy, did we fuss over her. The phones were out, the smiles were as wide as the Norfolk Broads. We had just finished third in the *Class 4 British Stallions Studs EBF Novice Stakes*. We had a brief chat with Jack and although I can remember telling him how pleased we were, I can't accurately recall what Jack said back. I think he made some observations about Free Love running around a bit when he gave her a tap, so he put his stick down fairly promptly. He had certainly given her a lovely ride. It looked to have been a really positive experience for her, which was the most important thing.

After a last round of pats and pictures, Free Love was led away and we went over to the owners and trainers' bar to buy Tom a drink. It's no exaggeration to say that I was elated. I was somewhere up in the heavens, and it would be a long time before my feet touched the ground. My mind was buzzing with the possibilities that lay ahead. We were now qualified for nursery handicaps which started in early July. I needed to go home and have a good look at the race but using Artair as a yardstick, I thought we might be handed a BHA rating of 68-72. We were on our way.

14 June 2018
Morning all. Free Love has eaten up and trotted up ok this morning. So pleased we are going in the right direction and hopefully we will be out on the racecourse again soon. All the best, Tom.

I replied saying that we were absolutely delighted with our filly's run. I sent a picture of a small article in the Racing Post which drew attention to the apparent draw bias at Yarmouth's two-day meeting. Apparently six of the seven races on the straight course were won by horses coming up the stands rail making Free Love's effort look even more gallant. I was already looking at options. There were novice races at Lingfield and Nottingham towards the end of the month, and one of the first nursery handicaps of the season was to be run at Lingfield on 11 July. The anticipation was draining, all-consuming and addictive. I was desperate to get that Yarmouth feeling again and couldn't wait to see our filly back in action.

22 June 2018

Joe finally finished his marathon GCSE exam schedule and I suggested we should make a visit to the stables to see Free Love. He'd missed out on everything so far and I knew from previous visits to Gary Moore's that he really enjoyed seeing the horses and talking to the people who looked after them. Gary's was a real family set-up and quite often a visit to Cisswood, near Horsham, would involve a chat with either Jamie or Josh, two of Gary's hardworking and talented jockey sons. I never saw Ryan there, but he did ride for Dad and when he was booked it was worth sitting up and taking notice. The strike rate was impressive.

I remember going to Cisswood one crisp morning at the tail-end of winter to watch a horse called Amen work. A share was available through Heart of the South and as I had just finished with one partnership, I was keen to take up a small stake in another. Josh was there nursing an injury and was happy to chat while the horses were working up the all-weather gallop. Flecks of snow were in the air as Amen effortlessly breezed by. He had athletic good looks and moved like a well-tuned sports car. I was tempted. He had cost an eye-watering 600,000 guineas as a yearling. By top stallion Galileo, out of Kitza, who had finished second in the Irish Oaks, Amen had an aristocratic pedigree. Yet Aidan O'Brien gave up on him after three poor runs in maiden company. He was then gelded, changed stables, and ran once over hurdles displaying only a scintilla of ability before Gary Moore took a chance on him for an undisclosed, but I imagine modest, sum.

I loved the horse. He was beautiful. And how good would it be to say that I owned a share in a horse by Galileo? And the dam? Oh yes, that's right, she was placed in an Irish Classic! For once, my head got the better of me and I declined, taking up a share that had become available in the rather more ordinary but tried and trusted handicapper, Good Luck Charm. Gary tried Amen over hurdles, on the flat and even experimented with steeplechasing. The best Amen managed before being given away as a riding horse, was a fourth place at Huntingdon which earned his new connections £239. How's that for a return on over 600 grand?

I had agreed with Tom to get to Wroughton House for 9am. We wanted to see Free Love work and Jackie had offered either 7.45am or 9am. I went for the latter which I thought might be less challenging for a sixteen-year-old who had just finished a punishing exam schedule and for the next few weeks was only interested in sleep, playing golf and watching the World Cup. He had my full support for those ambitions.

The sky was clear and the sun already warm on the skin when we left Dartford at around 7.30am. By the time we arrived at Newmarket it was obvious that another scorching day was on its way. Free Love did a steady canter and afterwards I took yet more pictures, this time of Jennie and Joe caressing our diminutive stable star. As usual, our little filly was docile and friendly. We all thought she would make a good family pet.

We had a chat with Tom who was typically generous with his time. He was keen for Free Love to run again quite soon now that she was beginning to blossom, and had looked at options at Lingfield and Windsor which were coming up within the next week or so. I knew I could make neither as we would be in Bordeaux for a few days around that time.

For nearly 30 years we could only take breaks during the school holidays. I went into teaching after working for ten years in the private and voluntary sectors and family holidays were therefore restricted by where we could afford to go in the cripplingly expensive month of August. We also had a big gap between Joe and his older siblings, which meant we were still tied to school holidays even though I had scaled down to a one day-a-week advisory role.

We thought that after the GCSEs there would be a golden opportunity to take off for a whole week at a quiet time of the year. How wrong could we be. Joe had sixth form induction days to attend, Jennie had various work commitments for her charity that couldn't be moved, and I was struggling with the early July schedule for my 'part-time' job which included the release of the Key Stage 2 SATs results and two important meetings of the school's Governing Body. In the end, we managed to find a narrow window of just four days when we could get away. The Lingfield and Windsor races both fell in that short period and I was resigned to missing Free Love's next race.

26 June 2018

Free Love was given an official BHA rating of 71. It was more or less what I expected and perhaps high enough for a small, relatively inexperienced filly who was about to embark on her handicapping career. On the other hand, Phoenix Star looked as if he could be quite useful and with the two expensive breeze-up purchases out the back at Yarmouth, it could be that the value of the race had been slightly underestimated. Only time would tell.

27 June 2018

Afternoon all, Free Love seems happy and well. Lingfield looks the weakest race and to give her he best opportunity we should go there this Saturday. Kerian O'Neil is booked to ride. The track and ground will suit. She had a nice form boost yesterday and I'm looking forward to running her. I'm going up to Newcastle on Saturday but all being well Jackie will be there. All the best, Tom

The form boost was Deputise's two-length victory in a Class 5 novice event at Wolverhampton. This expensive Kodiac colt had clearly learnt plenty from his racecourse debut and had taken a first small step towards justifying his 110,000 guineas price tag. It was encouraging to see a winner come out of the Yarmouth race as I was desperate to convince myself that that our effort to finish third was an achievement of heroic proportions. Lingfield looked a good opportunity and even though I was very disappointed at not being able to be there in person, I was awaiting the race with keen anticipation hoping that this really would be 'lift-off'.

30 June 2018

The Lingfield race was due off at 7.15pm and we were scheduled to arrive in Bordeaux around mid-afternoon, which would give me plenty of time to pick up the hire car, drive to our accommodation and work out the best way to watch the race live on my smartphone. Had Tom opted for Windsor on the following day, I might have had the tiniest of chances of getting there. I'd looked into the insane possibility of making a day trip from Bordeaux. Heathrow was the obvious airport and the times just about worked. It would have cost a fortune in flights though, not to mention how much the solicitors would charge to deal with the inevitable divorce proceedings that ensued.

We were all packed and ready to go when my phone buzzed alerting me to a WhatsApp message:

Good morning all, I hope you are well. Free Love has banged her off fore leg and subsequently has quite a lot of filling in it. She will be absolutely fine but won't be able to run this evening at Lingfield. She has had some anti-inflammatory treatment and can run again in five days (Nottingham amongst others looks a possible) all being well. Sorry to be the bearer of bad news, we will live to fight another day! I hope you all have a great weekend. All the best, Tom.

I had mixed feelings about the news. My first thought was for the filly. Tom seemed to be saying that this was a minor, even routine injury that would clear up very quickly. I hoped that was the case and she would soon recover with no harm done. If I'm honest, I was also relieved. I wouldn't miss out on seeing her run in the flesh. Selfish, I know, but the Free Love project had become an all-consuming passion. All the research, the admin, the financial planning, the stable visits and the progress bulletins, all led to the racecourse. Kieran was wrong. The fun started when they were racing.

5 July 2018

We had a fantastic time in southern France. It was blisteringly hot, making us grateful for choosing accommodation near Arcachon Bay rather than in the city. A day trip by train (Patrick and Mick would have been proud of me) was enough to take in the architectural splendour of Bordeaux. For the rest of the time we were happy swimming in the sea under the towering gaze of the remarkable Dune de Pilat. We even managed a flying visit to catch three races at La Teste de Buch racecourse on our way back to our holiday apartment where we witnessed the rarity of an England penalty shoot-out win. I'm not sure what our French neighbours thought of the racket being made by the three of us during our nail-biter against Columbia. I certainly won't have any difficulty remembering in years to come where I was when Jordan Pickford made that one-handed save and Eric Dier calmly slotted home the winning penalty.

9 July 2018

The four days in Bordeaux raced by and I was soon contemplating Free Love's next race, which Tom had decided should be the handicap at Lingfield rather than the novice event at Nottingham which looked a bit warm. Richard Fahey's Red Balloons would be a tough nut to crack. There was also Richard Hannon's More Than Likely who had won his last two and looked to be heading for Nottingham as well. We gave the race a swerve but Lingfield would mean another very long journey for Patrick and Mick.

The Lingfield handicap didn't appear to be a particularly strong contest. Free Love and Tarzan were the two highest rated horses, both with BHA ratings of 71. They would be joint top weights carrying 9st 7lbs. The jockey booking looked interesting. Tom had managed to get the rising star of the weighing room, David Egan, to take the ride. David had just lost his claim a day or two before following an incredibly successful start to the season. He was attracting plenty of media interest and all the top trainers had been bending over backwards to use him. It remained to be seen if he would still be popular now that his apprentice days were behind him and his weight allowance had disappeared.

Although it was great to have David Egan's services, he's naturally light and can ride at eight stone if needed. Even with a larger saddle and a cavalier attitude to that jam roly poly pudding the night before, he would only be able to weigh-out at 9st 7lbs by adding around a stone of lead to his saddle. Little Free Love would therefore end up carrying a fair amount of dead weight which was far from ideal.

10 July 2018

Free Love makes her nursery debut tomorrow at Lingfield. She has trained well since her last run and the form from both Yarmouth and Nottingham looks reasonable.

She carries top-weight tomorrow which is not ideal for a smallish filly but on the other hand, the handicapper thinks she is the best in the race.

Looking at the race, North Korea has been second on her last two starts and should give another good account. Tarzan was a winner and Redcar earlier this season but has to bounce back from a poor run at Brighton last month. I would hope she has the beating of Habanera and Wolstonbury on known form to date.

The unknown is All Back To Mine who has had three quietish runs and would expect to go much better now handicapping and Al Manhalah who is very well-bred and surely better than has shown to date.

I am off to Yarmouth tomorrow, but Jackie will be on hand to saddle. Very best of luck, Tom

I agreed with Tom's analysis of the race which he sent by email. Although joint top weight and already a winner, it was hard to fancy Tarzan after his most recent run at Brighton. North Korea had to go close. She had been runner-up in her last two starts, and although the Goodwood race was a seller, it was a Class 3 race worth nearly £10,000 to the winner. There were a couple of dark horses in there as well who looked capable of much better in time. One of them, Al Manhalah, cost 80,000 euros as a yearling and was being sent on this mission by the hugely successful Mark Johnston stable. That was a 550-mile round trip from Middleham in North Yorkshire for this 56-rated youngster to whom our 10,000 guineas filly would be conceding over a stone. It looked a winning opportunity though, and I had a really good feeling that this was where the Free Love story was about to begin.

10 Lingfield

11 July 2018

No full-house. Mick declined my offer to stay overnight as he was involved with some outreach work that his church was undertaking with homeless people in York and needed to be on duty early on Thursday morning. However, he worked out that a day return by train was just about possible. Patrick was able to join him. That was the North bit of the partnership sorted. Trevor and I were both fine, but Pete was visiting family in Canada so his earlier Lingfield loss became my gain. Pete offered his owner's badge to his eldest son, Tom, who was able to get away from work to attend. I think he was going to take the afternoon off anyway as England were due to play Croatia in the World Cup semi-final later that evening.

I was confident. I was worried about the weight but felt that Free Love might be a cut above the opposition and was capable of running to an official rating of 75 or thereabouts. I had my maximum bet of £50 – a sum I've wagered only three or four times before. I secured 5/1 which I thought was a very fair price. An hour before the off, Free Love was 9/4 favourite.

Jackie was there to look after us. She was doing her level best to look after Free Love as well, making sure that the saddle with all its extra lead weight was put on as late as possible. As a result, Free Love was one of the last to enter the paddock. David Egan confidently introduced himself and we congratulated him on riding out his claim and on the way the season was going for him in general. Tom had obviously talked things through with Jackie and David and the plan was to be held-up in touch just behind the pace. North Korea looked sure to make the running.

The betting marking was doing strange things. Having been as low as 2/1 at one point, Free Love drifted back out to 4/1 as money came for North Korea and the lightly raced All Back To Mine who was ridden by David's dad, the well respected and very experienced John Egan. Although I am very much a small stakes punter, I'm not in the least bit sanctimonious about betting. It's an integral part of horse racing and always has been. Somebody, whose name evades me, once observed that horse racing without betting is hypocritical cant. I wouldn't go that far. But my passion for ownership has absolutely nothing to do with gambling. In fact, as I stood on the grandstand steps at Lingfield watching Free Love canter down to the start, the thought did cross my mind that having £50 on my own horse was a futile gesture given the sums of money involved to buy our filly and keep her in training.

It was a fleeting thought and I wasn't dwelling on it as Free Love entered the starting stalls. She had an ideal draw in four and as the gates opened and North Korea shot out like a ballistic missile from Pyongyang, our filly was able to tuck in behind just a couple of lengths off the pace. She seemed keen enough, but it was nothing like Yarmouth where for nearly half the race she pulled Jack Mitchell's arms out.

As the field approached the two-furlong marker, North Korea continued to blaze a trail with Tarzan showing good pace on the stands rail and All Back To Mine in contention on the far side. The riders were now becoming more animated, pushing away and asking their mounts to make a final effort as the furlong pole loomed. We were fourth, still with a couple of lengths to make up. Here we come! And then nothing. The effort was there but so was the anchoring weight. Free Love couldn't make up the ground and plugged on to finish fourth the same two lengths or so behind North Korea, who passed the post with a length to spare over All Back To Mine.

It was a deflating experience and I couldn't hide my disappointment. I really thought we were better than that. The race didn't look the strongest and despite carrying top weight, I had hoped to see Free Love race with a bit more dash and was despondent at the sight of her struggling to reel in what were probably some very moderate horses, albeit giving them weight. It was a quiet and sombre walk to back of the stands where the horses returned after racing.

Only the first three home are accommodated in the winners' enclosure at Lingfield, so we were in an area to the left of the paddock where the also-rans congregated. David said something about the ground being quick enough – the hot spell showed no sign of breaking. He may have mentioned needing a stiffer track. The weight concession would also have been raised. Most loyal owners are keen to consider any factor that could account for their horse not winning or running as well as it should. The going, track, distance, pace of the race, draw, interference suffered and so on and so on, are all held up as plausible reasons for the performance, or rather lack of performance. Several horses running faster than your one is never considered as valid though. But on this occasion, that's how it looked to me. We had every chance but came up short.

Seeing Free Love close up after her exertions lifted the mood. The one thing she had looked was genuine. She really had tried. There she was, hot and sweating, ears pricked and happy to have her small group of owners clustered around her, smiling through another round of photos. After all, this was our horse and we were her proud band of owners. Anyway, what did we expect off top-weight, our little filly giving pounds, even stones, away to everything else? And that ground was pretty quick out there. She would learn to settle better in time as well. Maybe a slightly stiffer track would suit? And at the weights, she still came out as the best horse in the race. There was no cause to be downhearted, I told myself. But my silent exhortation lacked conviction.

12 July 2018

Jackie must have picked up on the downbeat mood in the camp after the race as Tom had been very quick to send an encouraging message: *Good afternoon all. I was really pleased with Free Love's run at Lingfield today. She again shaped with plenty of promise for the future and there are loads of positives to take out of the race. She had to give an awful lot of weight away and probably wants a stiffer 5 furlongs. As I'm sure you all know these 5-furlong races often have to fall for you slightly. I'll let you know how she is in the morning, fingers crossed she's okay after running on that quick ground and we can make another plan soon. All the best, Tom.*

He was right, of course, and yesterday's effort was perfectly decent in the context of the race. The next day, a further message confirmed that Free Love had eaten up and was sound, showing no ill effects of racing on ground that had been plenty firm enough.

My disappointment wasn't with Free Love. Here was this small and relatively cheaply bought filly doing her level best to run as fast as she could less than three months after her second birthday. You couldn't fault her, and I loved having her as our horse. The disappointment was in the fading of the dream. The unrealistic hope of unearthing a rags to riches champion usually recedes with every run that a young horse has. Some horses can improve quite dramatically with racing, but most establish a fairly fixed mark of ability once they have had half a dozen runs under their belts. Yesterday we weren't good enough to win off a rating of 71. What did that mean for the future? Were we close to establishing a fixed mark of around 65? If so, we would be racing for pitiful prize money in low-grade handicaps at some of the country's smaller tracks.

All along I had hoped that Free Love would end up as a consistent 70-80 rated sprinter (while secretly dreaming of much more). At this rate the filters on the BHA race search facility would need to be set differently. No point looking at listed or Class 2 conditions races anymore. No point looking at Class 3 and 4 handicaps. No point at looking at any race with prize money of much more that £3,500 to the winner. No point in thinking that The North South Syndicate would have any choice other than to send Free Love to the horses in training sale in October. It wasn't a disaster – England delivered that yesterday evening against Croatia in the semi-final – but it wasn't looking great either. But I needed to remember that yesterday was only the fourth run of our filly's life. There was still time for her to improve and it was important to keep travelling in hope.

17 July 2018

The handicapper reacted to Free Love's Lingfield run by easing her rating down two pounds to 69. It was a cautious drop as over sprint distances I've always used the rule of thumb of around 3lbs equating to a length. On that basis we would need to meet North Korea on around 7-8lbs better terms to have a chance of getting level with her. As North Korea was put up 4lbs for winning, it meant that if we raced against each other tomorrow, both horses would carry exactly the same weight, representing a 6lbs turnaround in our favour compared with Lingfield. It seemed fair enough, I thought.

I had already been looking at the possibilities for our next run. Because auction races were out, it seemed sensible to stick to nursery handicaps for the time being. Races at Sandown and Wolverhampton at the beginning of August fitted the bill as did a median auction race at Chester around the same time. We were still qualified to run in the latter as it was the average price fetched at auction by the sire's progeny that determined eligibility.

Wolverhampton would probably be a weaker race but there was no doubting the appeal of having a runner at Sandown Park which is, on balance, my favourite racecourse in the country. The viewing is fantastic and the parade ring, with its elegant surrounding lawns, just perfect for a summer evening meeting, especially if the sun is shining.

21 July 2018

I found myself in Ireland. More to the point, I found myself at Brian McElhinney's 60th birthday party in Ennis, County Clare. I had not exchanged a single word with 'The Judge' for the best part of forty years, until one of my secondary school contemporaries decided that he'd organise a school reunion. The first gathering was a low-key affair at The Alma in Sidcup, about half a dozen years ago. One or two of the boys were still in touch with each other but for many it was a first encounter since school days.

The Alma was one of the closest pubs to the school and some of us used it as a local for a while, especially as it had a full-size snooker table in a back room that was really popular with a number of regulars, young and not so young. I spent many happy hours playing bad snooker and chatting away with friends over a pint. Patrick was a frequent user as was Ray Gately who featured in that traumatic first football match for Old St Mary's FC. Ray was the one wearing the Argentina top.

You could find love in The Alma as well. I met Jennie there. She had left school at sixteen but, after five years of work, decided she wanted to steer her career in a more interesting direction. She was working as a part-time barmaid in the pub while studying at the London College of Printing in the Elephant and Castle. The qualification she gained helped her to have a rewarding career in publications and marketing. She's bright girl, Jennie. She always plays each-way on the Tote when we go racing. Sometimes it's a place only bet. When I tell her how unlucky I was to have backed that 16/1 shot who was beaten a short-head, she knows how I will answer her enquiry about whether I backed the horse each-way. With silence.

Simon Ross, the sociable and optimistic organiser, was adamant that the first reunion in the Alma should not be the last and he set about making it a biannual event. I missed at least one of them but made a point of getting to the gathering held at Sidcup Rugby Club in February 2017. St Mary's was a rugby school and a number of the boys joined Sidcup RFC when they left, some of them playing at a very decent standard for the first team. This reunion was timed to coincide with England's Six Nations game against Wales which was shown on a big screen in the large bar. I wasn't sure I could make all of it but decided I should get there at least for a drink, especially as the email trail revealed that Brian was going to make a weekend of it in London and intended to get to the rugby club by early evening.

I had no idea whether Brian had kept up his interest in horse racing, but I thought it would be strange if he hadn't. He had always considered himself Irish and had moved back 'home' around 30 years ago. That much I knew. Avoiding an interest in horse racing while living in Ireland would take some doing.

I needn't have worried. Brian hadn't changed very much at all. I recognised him immediately. He still looked strong and powerful enough to carry an A Level maths text book or two, and our conversation was soon on the subject of horses. Brian had also become involved in partnerships, though on a more expansive scale. He had obviously done well since switching horses in mid-race to train as a pharmacist, which was his dad's line of business. Things seemed to have worked out very well for Brian and I was delighted for him.

At the reunion, I reminded Brian of the day his dad took us to Lingfield for a jumps meeting. It was my first ever visit to a racecourse. It all looks so neat and ordered on the television, but when you're there, it's mud-splattered, steaming and visceral. I'll never forget the excitement of that wet afternoon in Surrey in the autumn of 1974.

England beat Wales, and as the St Mary's alumni departed, Brian and I agreed to stay in touch, which is easily said but rarely done. It's more likely to happen when there's a good incentive to keep communicating. We had no trouble finding one and exchanged horse racing updates via Messenger and even had a tipsters' championship during the Cheltenham Festival. Just like old times, The Magician and The Judge locking horns again. Another rarity was me taking up a later offer from Brian to drop in on his 60th birthday bash if we found ourselves in Ireland towards the end of July. Me, Jennie and Joe made a three-day break of it having a great time at the 60th birthday party which also celebrated 30 years since Brian and his wife, Jenny, returned to the homeland.

The trip included a visit to Galway to catch up with another great racing pal, Ray Gately, who often pops over for York in August and stays a night or two with me before flying back to Shannon. Like Brian, Ray returned 'home' after growing up and working in England. His parents were originally from Loughrea and that's where he settled after finishing with primary school headship in Sussex, eventually becoming a hospital chaplain in Galway.

Ray has enthusiastically embraced all aspects of Irish life. He's the type of person who will talk to anyone and, as a result, is known by almost everybody. And that Argentina shirt? Ray shares that irritating Irish trait of supporting whoever England are playing against. The 10-0 drubbing for the football team featured Ray wearing his 'hand of God' top which was, allegedly, as close as he could get to white. He had no problem with the orange, green and white strip which I bought in Welling soon afterwards. I told him it was the cheapest combination I could get, but he would have none of it. As far as Ray was concerned, it was only natural that Old St Mary's FC should run onto the pitch sporting the Irish Tricolour.

It was a lovely short holiday during which we caught up with some old friends and met some new ones as well. Brian was interested to hear about Free Love's progress, and I said that I would keep the updates coming. When we returned to England two days later, it was time to think about entries.

30 July 2018

We opted for Sandown. Tom was pleased with Free Love's recent work and in the end decided to keep her on a straight course. After the horror show of Kempton, we were all happy with that decision. Mick couldn't make any of the shortlisted races as he was in the States visiting family but the rest of us could get there, including Patrick who was due to officially retire the day before the Sandown race. What a way to start a life of leisure!

The field looked strong. Paul Cole's Li Kui had been deemed good enough to take his chance in Royal Ascot's Windsor Castle Stakes following his maiden win at Catterick. He failed to trouble the judge but his official rating of 75 didn't look too harsh. Amanda Perrett's Tinto had progressed nicely in his three runs to date and now made his handicap debut. One with a similar profile, who really caught the eye, was Clive Cox's 50,000 guineas Dark Angel colt, Dark Shadow. He looked sure to start favourite off an opening handicap mark of 74. It made me realise how badly handicapped we might be as the 5lbs Dark Shadow had to concede to Free Love was only the same as the fillies' weight allowance she would get in a conditions race. This was going to be a tough task, there was no doubt about that.

11 Sandown

1 August 2018

The long, hot summer continued, and it was a beautiful evening at the Esher track. It was a music night and there was a huge, youngish crowd pulled in by the attraction of George Ezra and band playing an hour-long set after the racing finished. Trevor is a very accomplished musician and his four children have all followed in a similar vein. One of them, James, has even made a living out of music and it was by sheer coincidence that he was on duty at Sandown as the musical director and keyboard player for George Ezra.

But that wasn't the big news of the evening. I went with Jennie and Joe and we got there in plenty of time. We took full advantage of the excellent hospitality that Sandown offers its visiting owners and made ourselves comfortable at a shaded table on the lawn just outside the lounge. Patrick was coming by train and appeared to be cutting it quite fine. There was no point phoning though. His ancient mobile never seemed to be switched on but I was confident he would make it.

Suddenly, like the mesmerising opening scene in David Lean's Lawrence of Arabia, Patrick appeared in the distance, a fairer, slightly more mature Omar Sharif whose entrance would be a life-changing event for the group. As he drew closer and it was possible to distinguish the detail of his features and clothes, it became apparent that he was carrying a small object. It was slim, rectangular and black. Patrick had a smartphone!

We congratulated Patrick on his retirement and the acquisition of his new gadget. But it was very much one step at a time. He was able to use it to make calls and texts but when questioned about WhatsApp, or any other app for that matter, all semblance of understanding vanished from his face. He would need to get Sally to guide him on the next steps of his journey down the digital superhighway.

It was time to go to the pre-parade ring where Free Love would be saddled. At Sandown, this paddock is tucked away in a quiet tree-lined space which attracts just a handful of watchers. We were in the centre looking on as our filly was led round. She looked in really good shape, her summer coat shining in the evening sun. All was calm until one of the other runners seemed to get spooked and became quite fractious. His behaviour had a knock-on effect and Free Love backed away and became a bit stirred up. She seemed to be calm enough when she entered the main paddock but given that she had been a bit keen in the early part of her last two races and we were trying to get her to settle better and conserve energy, we could have done without the antics of the other horse.

Jack Mitchell was back in the saddle. Tom was there and although he felt that Sandown's stiff five furlongs, which was steadily uphill throughout, might suit Free Love, he was keen that she should be given a chance to settle in the hope that there would be something left at the business end of the race. As Jack was given the leg-up, Free Love looked a little bit lit-up and on the way to the start her jockey had to keep a good hold of her. She seemed to be in a hurry get on with things.

As we walked to the grandstand, I had a chat with Tom about Lingfield. I explained that my initial disappointment was to do with the realisation that Free Love wasn't going to reach a similar level of form as her full-brother and sister. After all, they had both won early in their two-year-old careers and ended up being rated in the mid-70s. I told Tom that we would be very happy if Free Love achieved that sort of rating and he pointed out that it was still possible for the filly to do so. We just needed to take it one race at a time.

Our draw was no help. There were only seven runners and we were in stall seven. I knew that high draws can be difficult to overcome on Sandown's five-furlong course but with a relatively small field that needn't be a problem. The worry was being on the wide outside and not being able to find cover behind other horses. It all depended on the start.

Free Love seemed to have calmed down by the time the runners reached the stalls and was last to be loaded. If she went in like a lamb, she roared out like a lioness. She absolutely pinged the start and Jack found himself in front on the outside within a matter of yards. Only Tinto on the rail matched strides with our filly, who was pulling fiercely, her head jerking violently from side to side. Tinto showed no signs of wanting to go on and with nothing else racing to the fore, we ended up sharing the lead until the halfway stage where Li Kui loomed up on the other side of Free Love.

From the two-furlong marker to the final furlong pole, Free Love and Li Kui were really racing. The favourite, Dark Shadow, who had been backed as if defeat was out of the question, looked momentarily in trouble as the two pacemakers fought out their private duel. However, within seconds, the complexion of the race completely changed. Dark Shadow found his feet and came with a surging run that saw him forge clear in the last 100 yards. As he made his move, Free Love's effort faltered. She weakened quickly and faded into sixth place, just under eight lengths behind the impressive winner.

I had felt the very briefest moment of hope as Free Loved raced head-to-head with Li Kui, but as she weakened, I berated myself for the naivety of that optimism. I knew after a furlong that she couldn't win in that class, on this course, behaving the way she did. She was burning up energy and her rapid retreat in the final part of the race was depressingly predictable. I had even said to Jack in the paddock that if the filly got out well perhaps it would be better to let her have her head and try to make all. Tom was always against that tactic as he felt she would just run fast before falling into a hole. He was right. Free Love might never win a race unless she calmed down and learned how to settle, even over sprint distances.

The runners filed back toward the winners' enclosure via the rhododendron walk. For those outside the first four, a space under a cluster of large trees at the top of the walkway is set aside to cool the horses down and allow owners, trainers and jockeys to have their earnest looking debriefs. Free Love was still breathing heavily after her exertions. I'm sure she appreciated the bucket or two of water that was splashed over her steaming coat. I looked on, feeling that more cold water had also been thrown over my dreams and aspirations.

Jack hopped off and was clearly not as downcast as his owners. He said what we already knew, that Free Love started almost too well and couldn't get cover from her outside draw. As a result, she pulled far too hard in the early stages of the race. We knew all that. But he added that, compared to Yarmouth, she felt like a different horse as she contested the lead with Li Kui for the best part of two furlongs. He thought our filly put her head down and really raced, knowing much more about what was expected of her. A chink of light, then.

We went through the usual post-race ritual of thanking Jack before he made his way down the slope to the weighing room. The mobile phones were out, and Free Love was being patted and talked to in encouraging tones. Of course she was a good girl, I told her. She just needed to get rid of some of that fizz.

I had a word with Tom and told him that I wasn't sure where we should go next. Free Love might get away with making all the running in a Class 6 race on an easy track, but we agreed that it would be better if she learned to settle. Tom said that we could consider sellers but quickly added, when he saw the look of dread on my face, that we could always buy her back. It was all about trying to find a race that she could win, however small that might be.

6 August 2017

It was clear, that after five runs, the future for the North South Syndicate was looking bleak. Money was pouring out of our racing account and the motivation to keep shoring it up wasn't being provided by Free Love's exploits on the track. I didn't need a crystal ball to see the future. Even if things improved, it was hard to imagine all five of us signing up for anything beyond our agreed October finish date, let alone another season. I had talked informally with the others about the possibility of bringing other owners into the syndicate if we needed to reduce our personal costs. This was something to think about for next season, perhaps. Eight to ten members would still be a small enough group for ownership to feel personal and it would obviously halve the financial burden currently being shouldered by the five of us. We knew people who might be interested in taking a share in a horse, but would they be interested in a 65 rated maiden?

There was another way to reduce overheads. Move Free Love out of Newmarket. It was something that I was now beginning to consider. A day earlier, I had paid the July invoice which was pretty steep. It had included farrier's fees for racing plates, transport costs to Lingfield and 31 days of training fees at the full daily rate. The BHA invoice for the same month showed the mandatory deductions for the race entry fee and jockey booking. It also included a heath tax of £125 which is charged monthly for all horses who are trained at Newmarket and have access to its extensive gallops, the upkeep of which is the responsibility of the Jockey Club Estates. It confirmed what I already knew. Newmarket is an expensive place to have a horse in training. Not only do owners pay for the use of its facilities, they also pay for the kudos of being there.

I decided to investigate options that hit two targets. First of all, we had to get monthly training costs down by moving away from headquarters. Secondly, we needed to relocate somewhere that was more central. I couldn't see Patrick and Mick wanting to continue or having the enthusiasm to recruit new partners from their neck of the woods, if our horse raced almost exclusively at Lingfield, Kempton, Yarmouth, Sandown and all the other southern tracks within the orbit of Newmarket.

I did a little research, not much admittedly, and pinged off a speculative email to Mick Appleby who trains near Oakham in Rutland. I didn't want to identify our horse or the trainer looking after her. I simply said that we had a two-year-old filly who was racing and qualified for nursery handicaps, and we were thinking of moving her because of the expense involved with being based in Newmarket. I received a prompt response and the figures looked encouraging. I calculated that with a daily rate that was £10 lower than Tom's (and Tom wasn't an expensive Newmarket trainer by any means), lower race-day transport costs, and the absence of a heath tax, it would be around £400 - £500 a month cheaper to have Free Loved trained in Oakham. The email from Mick's secretary confirmed that there was a box available for our filly if we decided to go ahead with the move.

Why Mick Appleby? Well I knew of Mick's success on the all-weather circuit and the fact that he often bought cheaply and shrewdly at horses in training sales such as the big ones at Tattersalls in July and October. He has a reputation for being able to improve 'cast-offs' from big owners and stables. He was about six years ahead of Tom, having started training in 2010. Three winners in his first year jumped to 15 in the following one and the trajectory has been unrelentingly upward ever since. It looked as if Mick wouldn't be far off 100 winners in 2018. And the exact distances between Mick's stables at Langham and the members of the North South Syndicate? According to Google Maps, to York 112 miles, to Dartford 117 miles. You couldn't get much fairer than that.

7 August 2018

A few days earlier, Tom confirmed that Free Love had eaten up and was sound after the Sandown race. He said he would be in touch with a plan, but I thought I needed to make a personal visit to discuss a future that would include Free Love going to the October Tattersalls horses in training sale which had an entry deadline of early September.

It was another short-sleeves day and Newmarket was again bathed in sunshine when I arrived. I had deliberately avoided early morning work and said to Tom that I'd turn up after the horses had been exercised and the yard was a bit quieter. We discussed race options over a cup of tea in Tom's small office which as usual was overflowing with racing tack, silks, equine catalogues and paperwork.

Tom observed that the hot summer might come to our aid. The extreme weather had been responsible for Bath racecourse losing several of its fixtures due to the unsafe state of the ground. Bath has no watering system and watching its last televised meeting was quite an extraordinary sight. The horses were galloping over parched, russet-brown grass. There wasn't a square inch of green to be seen. It was no surprise that Bath's racing was suspended until the rains returned. Its cancelled fixtures were being reallocated elsewhere which meant that there might be one or two unexpected opportunities coming our way. One was a nursery handicap but that went to Ffos Las which was even further away and Tom's generous offer to charge just petrol costs for the transport in an attempt to get that first win, were appreciated but not met with enthusiasm.

We wandered around the yard where Free Love was being looked after following her walk through the woods. She went out every day whether it was for a couple of canters, a fast piece of work or just a relaxing walk on the heath. There she stood, lovely and temperate, as I went over to give her a pat and have a friendly word in her pretty ear. The stable hand was taking off her saddle but, as he did, a bit of tack got caught around Free Love's hind legs. She immediately and unsuccessfully tried to kick it off and with the girth strap still stubbornly stuck, our gentle little filly reared away and kicked out hard. She spun round with her lad keeping hold of her, still trying to free the strap. It happened quickly and as I took evasive action another violent kick caught me on the left hand. If I had been an inch or two further away, I would have been missed completely. An inch or two nearer would have meant a visit to the local A&E. The strap was pulled free and Free Love was immediately calm. Maybe she just wanted to remind me that a powerful and explosive thoroughbred was never far beneath that docile and friendly demeanour.

I was nursing a bruised little finger as we returned to Tom's small office to mull things over. I felt we needed a run sooner rather than later, if only for educational purposes. There was a race at Chelmsford coming up that was probably too good for us, a Class 4 novice event worth over £7,000 to the winner. It meant going back to the all- weather and racing round a bend for the first time since Kempton, but it was local and would help build up experience. There was another race at the same track, a more suitable nursery handicap, towards the end of the month, and perhaps we could run in both? That might help to take the fizz out of the filly.

I couldn't leave without tackling the main purpose of my visit. I felt I had to forewarn Tom that the North South's Syndicate's days may be numbered. He fully understood. He knew that if we had a couple more unsuccessful runs and Free Love's rating nudged downwards towards 60, there would be no way that we could afford to keep her in training for another season. She would have to go to the sales, where she would be picked up for buttons, leaving me and the others with some great memories but no chance of having another go. If our pockets were bottomless and we could afford, just for fun, to keep a very moderate horse in training who had little prospect of winning any meaningful prize money – a win in a Class 6 handicap might cover one month's training expenses – we would carry on. But we couldn't, so it wasn't going to happen.

I wanted to keep going. I was desperate to carry on with the addiction of the adventure. I was deeply saddened by the thought that I was nearing the end of a project I had so keenly anticipated for such a long time. During those early years, when I was building up my love for the sport, not for one second did I think I would ever be in the middle of the parade ring looking out. I always thought I'd be a punter looking in, watching the owners, trainers and jockeys from afar, vicariously experiencing ownership by latching onto horses who became favourites or even heroes. That was the nearest I thought I would come to realising the dream, because in a funny way you owned your heroes. They belonged to you.

I mentioned to Tom that I had already thought about trying to get one or two more brave souls to join the partnership and by spreading the load we might have a chance of carrying on for longer. He accepted that it would be hard to do this if Free Love's form didn't improve. It costs about £2k a month to keep a horse in training whether it's rated 65 or 95. It might be hard to persuade friends that shelling out a chunky regular monthly payment for a filly who hasn't won a race, and is odds against winning one in the future, equates to having fun. Perhaps Kieran was right after all.

What I didn't have the heart to do was tell Tom about a possible stable move. At this stage it was just research. Anyway, there was the novice event at Chelmsford to have a crack at. Who knows what would happen there? Perhaps Free Love would turn a corner and the future of the venture would look much more positive. We would need to wait and see, but it wasn't only money that was running out. It was time as well.

Before I left Newmarket, I made a brief visit to the Palace House Museum. Ages ago, I had bought a discounted annual pass but never got around to using it. It took me a little while to pull up the email on my phone which confirmed the purchase, and even longer for the member of staff on the desk to match it with the museum's records. It was something I had organised shortly after I retired from headship and somehow, well over a year had disappeared since.

It wasn't an extensive visit. I didn't cross the road to see the collection of paintings, restricting myself to the main building which charted the history of horse racing and the development of Newmarket as a training centre. There were display cases of racing memorabilia housing ancient trophies, silks, fading photographs and handwritten ledgers. The sense of the past, both equine and human, was tangible.

The intriguing nature of Palace House failed to lift my spirits though, and I was soon back in the car for a solitary return journey to Dartford. It was a chance to think things through and consider what should happen next, other than ask the boys to put more money into the kitty. I estimated that we would need to contribute another £500 each. That, together with the next injection of cash from the VAT man, should just about give us enough to pay the August and September bills. It was two or three more runs, then off to the sales. But what about that stable move? Maybe that was the last roll of the dice to be made.

8 August 2018

I sent a pretty comprehensive email to the boys summing up our position:

Gents,

I'll apologise now for the length of this email, but the time is fast approaching when we need to make a decision about what to do with our filly. We initially signed up for a season with Free Love going to the sales in October unless we all agreed on a different course of action. Ideally, it would be best to meet in person to talk this one through, although I can't see that happening when we next run which looks like Chelmsford on Friday - Pete and I both away if that's the case.

Perhaps Trevor could swing a day's racing at York on either Wednesday or Thursday of 22/23 August which would make a team meeting possible? Patrick, Mick, me and Pete are all definitely going.

Anyway, the deadline for entering the October Tattersalls sale for horses in training is 10 September, although it is possible to withdraw from the sale if Free Love starts showing the type of form that encourages us to carry on. The four of us who went to Sandown were rather pessimistic about this as once again the filly pulled too hard and, on a stiff track against decent opposition, couldn't finish off her race.

I shared all this with Tom when I visited the stables today. He knows we need a couple of runs before 10 September if that is possible. Free Love looked really fresh, which her work rider confirmed. She even got a bit edgy afterwards and kicked out, catching my hand and narrowly missing Tom. She's certainly ready to race.

On to money, the situation is dire. I dropped in all the paperwork for the next VAT return when I was in Newmarket. We are owed around £1,600 but at the moment we have less than £300 in the account.

Newmarket is also proving to be an expensive place to have a horse trained. Monthly heath fees are £125, and I reckon the daily rate that Tom charges is a fair bit more than some northern/midland based trainers. I contacted Mick

Appleby who trains near Oakham and has done well with sprinters and cast-offs from other stables. I attach his fees.

It's still not too late to consider switching stables, to Mick Appleby or anybody else. We could decide that the last two months may as well be cheaper than what we are currently paying. And you never know, another trainer might just get that bit improvement out of Free Love that either lifts her price at the sales or encourages us to keep her in training for a bit, even if only until the February sales next year. Using last year's October sale results as a price guide, I think Free Love has a current residual value of around £3-6K.

Don't get me wrong. I don't regret taking a chance with Tom. His horses are well looked after and continue to run well. We have received great service and I can't see how Mick Appleby, who has over 100 horses in training, could spare me the time that Tom did this morning on the gallops and in the office afterwards. It's been the same for all of us when we either visited the yard or met him on the racecourse.

Anyway, there it is gents. We clearly need to talk. What about a trip to York, Trevor? I'm sure it would be good for the soul!
Regards, Tony

15 August 2018

Free Love was declared for the novice race at Chelmsford. It looked a tough assignment. Only nine stood their ground at the declaration stage but the field included three previous winners, Isaan Queen, Sparkalot and Autumn Splendour. However, the likely favourite looked to be David O'Meara's Lovin, a $60,000 USA bred filly who had run only once, finishing an excellent fifth of 17 in a competitive maiden race for fillies at Glorious Goodwood two weeks earlier. She seemed sure to start favourite with champion jockey, Silvestre De Sousa, booked to take the ride.

We were struggling to get our owners there. Patrick had visitors over the weekend, which ruled him out. Trevor's work made him a non-runner and Mick had commitments as well. Pete was good to go but I was camping in the delightful village of St Nicholas-at-Wade, near Broadstairs.

Our holidays aren't usually this disjointed, or frequent for that matter. It's just the way it worked out with Joe's GCSEs and Brian's 60th. We've camped at the same site three or four times before, mostly in August when there is a large and lively folk festival in Broadstairs. The town is really buzzing during that week and before you conjure up images of bearded men whining away while stuffing fingers in their ears, there's quite a bit of crossover music as well. There are also plenty of bearded folkie types, to be fair.

I love it down there. The beaches at Joss, Kingsgate and Botany Bay are lovely and unashamedly English in character. Reculver, with its ruined church perched on the end of the cliffs, is enchanting, reached by an invigorating cycle along the sea front. We can tow the caravan to this part of Kent in an hour.

Yes, a caravan. I'm not quite sure how we acquired a touring caravan. About twenty years ago, if you told me that not only would we possess one but love using it as well, I would have thought you mad. I didn't mind slumming it in a smart holiday cottage in Pembrokeshire or a farmhouse in Brittany, but camping? Anywhere with a mini-bar got the thumbs-up from me.

All that changed when Matt and Celia were old enough to take advantage of the facilities that French campsites have to offer. We tried one in Normandy which had static caravans to rent (mobile homes, I think they call them). They weren't cheap to get hold of in August but boy, were they comfortable. Hot and cold running water, no waste buckets to empty or water butts to fill. A dining area, a decked patio, a barbecue on the lawn. And comfortable beds. As for the children, they were forever in the swimming pool whizzing down the flumes.

These impeccably maintained campsites have tennis courts, cafes and restaurants. They are smart and embraced by the French, as well as plenty of families from Holland and Germany who roll up in their expensive camper vans and touring caravans. It's not a camping model that you see so much in England and, for that reason, if we're taking the van away in the UK, we're happy to find a nice green site with a decent shower block rather than look for a bigger one with a pool and other facilities. We don't seem to do that as well as the French, veering more towards Butlins than Eurocamp.

Anyway, our introduction to French camping prompted an impulse buy of a caravan. Jennie had received a rare bonus from Grant Thornton, her employer before she moved into the charity sector. It wasn't huge, but it was enough for us to think about buying a second-hand van. We bought a two-berth Sterling Europa and used the awning to create a second bedroom. Our first attempt to put together this large piece of tarpaulin and its baffling collection of metal poles took hours and hours and would probably make a good subject for a Mike Leigh play. But we got there in the end and now consider ourselves out of the novice stage. Class 5 handicappers, I'd say.

There we were at St Nicholas-at-Wade, camped up for a week, me and Jennie taking in the folk music while Joe and his schoolmate Marco played golf or amused themselves on the large grassy expanse of the campsite. Joe insists that he dislikes the caravan, but the truth is he dislikes not having company now his older brother and sister no longer holiday with us. Inviting Marco to come along was a winning move.

My first thought was that getting to Chelmsford would be difficult, but Joe's golf schedule came to the rescue. He was really keen to play in the junior open at Dartford on Friday and ages ago I promised him that I would run him there from St Nicholas-at-Wade if needs be. Here was the proposition I put to Jennie. We all return to Dartford on Thursday evening. Marco is dropped back home. We make sure our ancient cat, Misty, is surviving, do a bit of sorting out in the house and all sleep there that evening. On Friday, Joe is dropped off at the golf club while me and Jennie take off to Maldon for the day before going on to Chelmsford, where we would leave after our race, which was the first one on the card. I would book a table for 8.30pm at the Bell Inn at St Nicholas-at-Wade, where we would finish our holiday before towing the caravan back the next day. Joe could fend for himself for one night, I was sure.

The plan was approved. Chelmsford here we come!

Brave new world. Patrick gets a smartphone!

12 Chelmsford Part I

17 August 2018

Maldon was relaxing in late summer sunshine. The searing heat of June and July had passed but it was still a gorgeous, languid afternoon. We walked around the attractive and historic town, making a brief visit to the Maeldune Heritage Centre. The entrance is via what's left of St Peter's Church, which fell into disuse during the Reformation. Only the tower remains of this ancient place of worship. The extension, tacked on a couple of hundred years later, was the home of Maldon Grammar School for a while.

Inside the tower, a large embroidery, made to celebrate the 1,000th anniversary of the Battle of Maldon, was on display. It's a fantastic piece of local work, illustrating the town's history from the battle in 991, when the Saxons repelled a Viking invasion, to its 1,000th anniversary in 1991. It was nice to be unhurried and spend some time talking to the centre's volunteers about this vibrant record of local history, in which they took obvious civic pride.

The Blue Boar at the top of the high street also featured on our schedule. This fine old pub, which dates back to the 14th century, brews its own beer out the back in what used to be stables. The barrels of ale are racked up inside the bar and pints dispensed directly from there. I can highly recommend the produce of the Maldon Brewing Company.

The early afternoon was spent by the beautiful Heybridge Basin, a haven for wildlife and leisurely walkers. The basin was dug out of the marsh so that ships sailing down the Blackwater Estuary could enter the man-made waterway and unload their cargoes onto the barges heading inland to Chelmsford. Although the canal isn't used for commercial purposes anymore, it has discovered a new role, accommodating all sorts of leisure crafts. The trip around the Basin on an old sailing boat, with lunch and wine thrown in, looked appealing. Hiring the whole vessel for a private function looked even better.

The boat trip would have to wait for another day, and after a tranquil wander by the water, it was time to return to the car and set off for Chelmsford. Before we walked back up the hill, Jennie took a quick comfort break. Her timing was impeccable. The St Hugh's Stakes, a listed race at Newbury over five furlongs for two-year-old fillies, was due to go off. It was a race that I had reluctantly removed from my BHA searches, but after a cracking placed effort in a valuable nursery handicap, Tom had decided to let Gypsy Spirit take her chance.

I placed a pound on Heartwarming which enabled me to watch the race live on my mobile phone. It was another chance to reflect on how things had changed. Imagine being able to do that in 1974 when Sea Pigeon began his novice hurdling career. That was Star Trek technology. Archie Watson's Shumookhi won easily with Heartwarming a respectable three lengths back in second. However, it was Gypsy Spirit who commanded my attention. I could clearly see her on my phone's small screen battling on gamely to finish fourth, just a head away from third place and coveted 'black type'. Free Love and Gypsy Spirit really had gone their very separate ways. I was delighted for Tom, but I had to admit to another twinge of envy.

I was not prepared to take any chances with the traffic and made sure we were approaching the car at around 3.30, well over two hours before our race. My phone buzzed. It was Pete, telling me that he had spent 45 minutes almost motionless on the Princes Road which leads to the approach to the Dartford crossing. Friday night snarl-ups are all too common-place at what must be the busiest river crossing in Europe. When the tunnel and the bridge are struggling, the whole town chokes to a congested halt. Pete was smack-bang in the middle of one of those Fridays and was beginning to doubt that he would make it. As I drove to the racecourse, my phone buzzed again. Parked, I picked up a text from Pete saying that he had thrown in the towel and turned around to go home. He had managed about two miles in 90 minutes and the traffic news on the radio suggested it could take him the same time to cover the next two miles. Roll on the construction of the second crossing at Gravesend, which just might be completed before I go to meet my maker. I'd definitely only bet each-way on that outcome, though.

I was so glad that we got there. If I had decided that it really wasn't possible, or if Jennie had pulled a face at the proposal, Free Love would have run at Chelmsford without a single one of us to cheer her on and make a fuss over her afterwards. That wouldn't have looked too good as it was me who suggested to Tom that we should consider the race even though it wasn't a realistic winning opportunity.

There was plenty of time to relax in the small but smart owners and trainers' lounge which is sited above the paddock behind the main stand. We found a spare sofa on the balcony overlooking the parade ring and chatted with a very friendly couple who owned General Zoff, a three-year-old who appeared to be a promising young stayer. Stamina was also required of the General's owners as the two-mile handicap which he contested was the last race on the card, not due off until 9pm. I talked about our modest project and my thoughts about moving Free Love, making it clear that it wasn't anything to do with being unhappy with how Tom had treated us. Quite the reverse.

It was time to go and see my girl. We walked towards the pre-parade ring where Jackie appeared. Tom was still making his way back from Newbury. My hopes weren't high. The race looked hot enough and our cause wasn't helped by our draw which, for the second time running, put us widest of all. If a high draw at Sandown can sometimes be a disadvantage, it's always a negative at Chelmsford. In five-furlong races the horses turn sharply left less than a furlong after the start. You'd have to be some machine to ping out from stall nine and get far enough clear to then swerve over to the rails before the bend was upon you. And even if you could do that, the amount of energy expended in the early part of the race would probably produce a slow-motion finish as the petrol gauge read empty inside the final furlong.

I greeted Jackie and congratulated her on Gypsy Spirit's excellent effort in the listed race at Newbury. She had spotted this 6,000 guineas bargain at the Doncaster yearling sales, so there was extra satisfaction to be gained from her filly's performance. Free Love entered the paddock and once again looked in great shape. She seemed to be strengthening up. Or was that my imagination? She was still the same small bay filly that I had proudly held last October at Newmarket for my new owner photograph, but she looked a bit stronger, a little deeper in the girth.

Free Love had a new partner. Charlie Bishop took the ride and I had no complaints about that. Charlie had ridden his first Group One winner on Accidental Agent at Royal Ascot in June, and his career was really taking off. We had a brief chat about the Sandown fiasco and Charlie confirmed that he would try to drop in just behind the leaders accepting that the draw had done us no favours. In my mind's eye I saw the nightmare of Free Love trapped out wide, her head swinging violently from side to side as Charlie tried to restrain her and get in behind horses.

Not only did our filly look stronger and more mature, she was more relaxed as well. Just after Charlie got in the saddle, one of the lightly-raced colts started playing up quite badly, rearing up and forcing his jockey to jump off. I looked on, waiting for Free Love to react, but she ignored this little drama and carried on walking, ears pricked, giving the impression that she was beginning to get used to all this race-day malarkey.

Lovin was backed as if victory was a formality, just a stepping stone to greater things. Free Love had been dropped two pounds after Sandown and now had an official rating of 66, which couldn't possibly be good enough to win a race of this calibre. Autumn Splendour was already rated 82 and it looked to me that something would need to run to around 85 to win it. That was surely beyond our little filly, whatever stall she occupied. The public agreed and 33/1 was readily available with the on-course bookmakers.

The canter down to the start went smoothly and Free Love entered the stalls like an old hand. I knew we couldn't win but my obligatory fiver each-way was wagered anyway. There was always the secret but fading hope that something extraordinary might happen.

As the last runners were loaded, I reviewed my expectations. What did I think would happen and what was I hoping for? These might be two different things. Free Love was entitled to be well beaten but what I wanted was some encouragement, a ray of light. It would be good to see our filly settle better and cope with the tight, all-weather track. Perhaps we could beat a few home and not finish too far behind the winner. Maybe scrambling into fourth place was an outside possibility. After all, the three previous winners all had to give us weight and the colts had to concede a little bit more.

These were my fleeting, anxious thoughts as the yellow flag was raised. As soon as the stalls were open, the 6/4 favourite was out and vigorously urged into an early lead by Silvestre De Sousa. Free Love broke well but was wide with no chance of getting across. Charlie found it difficult to slot in behind as our filly was racing upsides Isaan Queen who had also started smartly. Lovin grabbed the rail, hampering another runner as she did, and turned the first bend in front. Free Love didn't appear to corner that well, remaining quite wide and, as the field straightened up for the short dash to the line, she was in sixth place about half a dozen lengths off the lead. What would she find? Charlie gave her a couple of taps and she kept on, passing one rival and getting pretty close to overhauling another. Lovin had flown and crossed the line a decisive two-and-a-half length winner, with Free Love in fifth beaten a total of 5½ lengths.

It was more or less what I had expected, which was, rather perversely, a fraction disappointing. On the one hand, Free Love had stuck to the task well and finished off her race much better than at Sandown where she weakened quickly after her early antics. On the other hand, she hadn't surged past toiling rivals to win going away and catapult herself into listed company. That dream was fading away, race by race. A film critic would have given the performance three stars. It was neither one thing nor the other.

I made my way back to the unsaddling enclosure with mixed feelings. I wasn't sure if I was trying to convince myself that this was a positive effort, but if you looked at it objectively - if that was possible - you'd have to say that it was. The winner was going on to better things. There was no doubt about that. Lovin had taken full advantage of the weight allowances she received and had clearly built on the promise shown on her racecourse debut at Goodwood. The three previous winners filled second, third and fourth places and we were only three-quarters of a length behind Sparkalot, who would surely be handed an official rating in the high seventies given that Autumn Splendour, who finished third, already had a mark of 82. That meant Free Love had run to about 67 from a disadvantageous draw. She had also kept on well all the way up the straight.

I was processing this information as I neared Jackie who was waiting for Charlie and Free Love to return. Charlie was fairly upbeat when he jumped off. He felt our little filly had run well from her poor draw and he might have been able to snatch fourth place if he had been really hard on her but didn't see the point in subjecting a young horse to such a draining experience. We were agreed on that last bit, but I'm not sure we could have finished any closer than we did given the quality of the opposition and the handicap of stall nine.

It was good that Free Love appeared to handle the tight bends and the all-weather surface well enough. After Kempton, there was always a nagging doubt about this. Coping with Chelmsford opened up more options for us. Settling better in the early part of the race was also a plus. Jackie felt Free Love was leading with the wrong leg round the turn (something missed by me) but was generally pleased with the filly's effort. All in all, there were more positives than negatives.

'What's she rated? 66 isn't it?' Charlie enquired as he fixed his gaze on Free Love, his saddle removed and draped over his left arm.

'She can win a nursery off that mark. Maybe two,' was our jockey's parting shot. It was confirmation of what a good booking this had been. Charlie Bishop was clearly going places.

18 August 2018

The run back to St Nicholas-at-Wade went smoothly and we were in The Bell Inn just after eight for our meal. The following morning, we took down the awning and did all the tasks needed to pack up and tow the caravan back home, where we would keep it on our drive for a day or two of cleaning before returning it to storage in Farningham.

During the morning, I had a chance to watch the race replay several times and take in what the Racing Post made of it all. The RP deemed yesterday's race to be a 'fair novice event' and felt that a RP rating of 82 for the winner was justified if the placed horses, who were all previous winners, were used as yardsticks. Free Love's comment was: *Held up, headway under pressure over 1f out, not trouble*

157

leaders. The in-depth analysis of the race didn't provide anything very insightful. All we got was a rather perfunctory: *Free Love ran okay considering she had a wider trip than ideal.*

If that analysis was a little underwhelming, so was the response from the others. Pete felt it was more of the same, which I thought was a little harsh. However, I couldn't argue that it still left us rated in the mid-sixties which wasn't what we had hoped for at the start of our adventure. Free Love had now run six times and her form figures read 883465. She had won just over £1k in prize money by virtue of her placed efforts at Yarmouth and Lingfield. Rather irritatingly, because the Chelmsford race was a non-handicap, prize money only extended to fourth place. There was no 'appearance money' for 5th – 8th places which was now a welcome feature of class 4, 5 and 6 handicaps. Just to run at Chelmsford had therefore cost us around £350 in entry, jockey and transport fees for zero return. Quite an expensive racecourse gallop.

Maybe an era in which only the very rich owned racehorses was better for the sport, was my self-pitying reflection. There is probably far too much racing taking place these days, most of it very moderate in nature. Yes, prize money is poor, but are we really expecting owners of 66 rated handicappers to be subsidised so that they can carry on with their expensive hobby for free? It's true that we need a large bunch of indifferent animals to keep the circus going at the likes of Wolverhampton, Southwell and Lingfield. That doesn't mean that the owners of these creatures have a right to lavish prize money pots and generous appearance money that arguably rewards failure. But it should be a bit better than it is. Win a race and earn enough money to pay for one month's training fees? That can't be right. Or maybe it can, and the likes of me should return to suburbia to run football teams, play bad golf, sort out photo albums in the garden, and watch the racing on TV, leaving the monied and the landed to look after the breed at their own considerable expense. Perhaps I was becoming just another self-pitying, whinging owner.

20 August 2018

The big York Ebor meeting was only two days away. I had planned to travel up with Pete very early on Wednesday morning. It was a tried and trusted routine. Leave at 6.30am, arrive at Patrick's house in York less than four hours later, leaving time to walk up to The Bar Convent near Micklegate where an excellent cooked breakfast was served in serene surroundings.

The Convent is a lovely old building, with beautifully tiled floors. Nowadays, you can stay there, book one of its conference rooms, visit the heritage centre or just wander in off the streets for a cup of tea and a moment of quiet reflection. Ray wasn't able to make it over from Ireland on this occasion, but had he been travelling with us he would have insisted on the Convent on the grounds that we would receive food for both body and soul - which could only help with the difficult task of picking winners.

I've been going to the big York August meeting on and off since 1980. Mostly on, I guess. The first time I went, a few of us rented a cottage in Masham. I can't remember the exact details, but I think me, Patrick and Tim were there. My memories of this holiday are hazy. I know it was Masham and not Magaluf, though. I also remember that we didn't have a car between us and had to make our way to the races by train, which discouraged us from attending on all three days.

In any event, I think we needed a break after day one on Tuesday, which was the only day in the British horseracing calendar that featured two Group 1 races – the Benson and Hedges Gold Cup (today known as The International Stakes) and the Yorkshire Oaks. I had three bankers and had the agonising experience of seeing them all beaten in second place. The flying Irish filly, Cairn Rouge, was out-battled by the ultra-tough Master Willie in the big race. About an hour later, Shoot A Line comprehensively outstayed Vielle in the Yorkshire Oaks, and to cap it all Glint Of Gold had his lustre tarnished in the Acomb Stakes by the 33/1 debutant Cocaine, who in later life became an inconsistent handicap hurdler. Glint of Gold followed a very different path, finishing second to Shergar in the following year's Derby before winning a number of group races over middle distances. I still can't work out how Cocaine beat him on that August afternoon in 1980. Perhaps the clue is in the name.

Mercifully, the disaster was short-lived. In blind loyalty to Sea Pigeon, I backed Shaftesbury at 12/1 for the following day's Ebor Handicap. Sea Pigeon had walked all over my selection in Redcar's Zetland Gold Cup, but I thought the longer trip would suit and reasoned that anything capable of chasing home the mighty Sea Pigeon must be pretty useful. Shaftesbury was an emphatic winner and I was back in the game.

I really can't recall much of what happened on the Thursday. I know I saw the great sprinter Sharpo win the first of his three Nunthorpe Stakes, but that's about all. But I do remember very clearly The White Bear in Masham and the fabulous Theakston's beers which were produced in the town by the family owned brewery. There have been acrimonious take-overs since, causing much consternation and tut-tutting amongst the real ale brigade, but in 1980 Theakston's Best bitter was group one class.

They were great times. And I was looking forward to another dose of the magic on Wednesday, when Roaring Lion was set to lock horns with Poet's Word in the International Stakes. But there was work to be done as well. It was time to make a decision about Free Love's future and in the email I sent later that day, I tried to be precise about the finances in the hope that when we met up, we would be able to decide there and then on our course of action:

Gents,

Trevor looks unlikely to be able to get to York on Wednesday but has said that he'll call to discuss matters with us if he can't be there in person. I thought it might be useful to give you all a review of our finances ahead of our discussions, but I'll bring all the paperwork with me anyway.

I think we should be realistic and plan for the worst, which would be that Free Love stays with Tom until the end of October, runs three more times and doesn't win any significant prize money. If she went to the sales as a 60 rated maiden, she'd fetch around 3,000 guineas.

There is another option. A move to Mick Appleby (or any other cheaper yard) at the end of this month would mean an overall reduction in costs for September and October of around £1200 based on a cheaper daily stabling rate, lower travel costs to races and no heath fees to pay. It also opens up a few more options for us. For example, there is a 0-75 nursery at Catterick in September that is far less travel for the filly if based at Oakham. It also provides the potential to keep the partnership going for a few months more on the all-weather circuit for those who want to (there are sales for horses in training in February) as we could probably get a few more to join the syndicate with the incentive of keenly priced stabling fees.

All this needs to be talked about. The agreement which we all signed up to states that the filly goes to the sales unless we ALL agree on another course of action. I look forward to seeing you on Wednesday.

Regards, Tony

22 August 2018

Stay with Tom or move to Mick. An entry for the October horses in training sale was a given, wherever we were. These were things to discuss with Pete on our journey to York, which started promptly at 6.30am.

Pete was initially shocked at my suggested departure time but reluctantly agreed once I reminded him of his recent nightmare on Princes Road. A good name for a film, I thought. It was his turn to drive so I was the navigator and talking form book. A Racing Post had been purchased, and Pete had his usual bags of lemon sherbets and wine gums in the glove compartment. I brought the bananas. You could run a Polar expedition with these resources.

What the expedition didn't need was more motorway congestion. Google Maps showed an emerging problem on the M11. The Dartford Crossing was clear, but as we approached it, traffic updates confirmed that the M11 northbound was closed due to an accident. The advice was to take the scenic route through Essex to avoid the stricken section of the motorway. It was estimated that this would put an hour on our journey.

What a pain, and how thoroughly predictable, I thought. I'm sure it was a serious incident. I'm equally sure that it needed a big emergency services operation, but motorway closures seem so commonplace now. Quite often there doesn't appear to be any real effort to get at least one lane open so that people with important work appointments, funerals to attend, planes to catch, and maternity wards to reach, aren't unreasonably inconvenienced. There are also racegoers to consider who want a fry-up and a pint before they reach the parade ring. These things irritate more with age. I was probably being unreasonably cantankerous, and after muttering a few mild profanities which made me feel marginally better, I concentrated on navigating us back onto the top of the M11 and from there to the A1.

Once on the A1, it was more or less plain sailing. I asked Pete for his thoughts on Free Love's recent Chelmsford run. He exuded ambivalence. I tried to remain objective but found myself talking up the performance. I felt I had to defend our filly and ended up describing her fifth place from a bad draw in almost heroic terms. The BHA handicapper was on Pete's side. Free Love had been eased down a pound to 65 in yesterday's weekly reassessments. I also quizzed Pete about our options. He seemed to favour a move if only to save some money before the inevitable fire-sale in October. I got the distinct impression that he felt it was now all about cutting our losses. To be fair, the evidence suggested that he was right. There was little point banging on about Free Love's pedigree and the exploits of her brother and sister. She hadn't displayed the same precociousness and had only hinted at reaching a level of form within touching distance of her siblings. I still thought she would win a race, but it might be next year and a very lowly one at that. If that was the case, we wouldn't be hanging around waiting for it to happen.

We lost about an hour and a half in total and arrived in York at 11.30. There was no time for a leisurely breakfast. We parked up outside Patrick's and within minutes we were walking with him to the York Brewery tap where we had arranged to meet Mick. Kieran and his brother John would also be there. My younger brother, another Pete, trained it over from Manchester for the day. He's not a fan but enjoys the occasional day at the races and the banter and beer that goes with it.

It was a familiar annual event. Old friends, a pint of Terrier, lots of leg-pulling about what we fancied for the big race, and a tipsters' championship which involved everyone choosing a name then selecting a horse in each race. The stake was £2 a head. It had remained £1 for about twenty years until quite recently when Patrick boldly and controversially suggested it was time for it to be increased. His proposal sneaked through by thin majority. Our tipsters' names changed on an annual basis depending on what was going on in our lives. Patrick plumped for The Retiree. I went for The Executive Head. I think Kieran went for Solfeggio, a filly trained by Chris Wall in which he had recently acquired a 10% share. I can't remember the other names, but we had a field of seven so there was £14 up for grabs. I had to remind the winner that it was all about the glory and not the vulgar cash as I begrudgingly handed over my £2 after the last race.

As usual, the racing that day was top class. Roaring Lion was a spectacular winner of the International, and Phoenix Of Spain looked above average when scything through the Acomb Stakes opposition. The crowd didn't feel as big as last year and nowhere near the numbers that crammed into every corner of the course to watch the unbeaten Frankel power home by seven lengths in the 2012 International Stakes. It was relatively easy to get to the paddock and make it to the top of the grandstand, even if the ascent was tackled only minutes before the off. Once up there, I was reminded why I love York. The track is a huge, sweeping gallop, its home straight wide and flat enough to make hard luck stories a rarity. The sky over the Knavesmire seems to go on forever and the sense of space inspires awe and wonder, as we primary school teachers would say.

After the racing, it was back to Patrick's for a cup of tea and our conference about Free Love's future. I had kept all the paperwork relating to our filly in a single A4 lever arch file. It contained BHA invoices, monthly training bills, bank statements and registration documents. Me, Pete, Patrick and Mick sat down to consider the evidence. By now, we knew that Free Love had been entered for the nursery handicap at Chelmsford next Tuesday. This had been discussed with Tom and had been anticipated. Unless something went amiss, we would be running.

It soon became apparent that everyone thought a move was the best way forward. Nobody was unhappy with how Tom had handled the filly, or the way in which he had communicated with us, but it was all about the future and we felt that this wouldn't be at

Newmarket. The only thing that would prevent an immediate switch of stables was the unlikely event of Free Love bolting up at Chelmsford next week. This would cause a delay but no more than that. When everyone looked at the bills, we concluded that we needed a cheaper training centre and maybe more syndicate members as well if we wanted to carry on.

I was asked why I had put forward Mick Appleby. I had to admit that it wasn't because of extensive research. I told the others that I looked at trainers based in the Midlands and Mick popped up. I knew a bit about him already and didn't look any further once my digging confirmed his all-weather prowess and his reputation for buying cheaply and improving horses. In the absence of any other suggestions, we agreed that it should be Mick and only a resounding win at Chelmsford would prompt a hasty change of plan. I agreed that I would make all the necessary arrangements with Mick and tell Tom shortly after Chelmsford that we were moving Free Love. The die was cast. But the deed was not yet done. The difficult task of telling Tom still lay ahead.

26 August 2018

The Chelmsford race closed at 10am. Minutes later the runners and draw were available. Eight horses would go to post. And the draw? We were out in stall eight. What were the odds on that happening? Precisely 504/1, I believe. Three races, three highest, widest, worst draws of all. It wasn't the day to buy a lottery ticket. What do the French say? *Jamais deux sans trois.* Things always happen in threes. Three low draws for Free Love and three wins would have been a more welcome *jamais deux sans trois*.

One horse stood out. Prince Of Rome trained by Richard Hughes had course and distance form, having chased home Quiet Endeavour in June. Quiet Endeavour had since gone on to rattle up a hat-trick of wins and was now rated in excess of 100. That made Prince Of Rome look pretty well in off a mark of 72, conceding just seven pounds to our little filly. One again it seemed depressingly easy to identify who was going to beat us.

I posted an exasperated message on our WhatsApp group saying that we might need to resort to bribery in future if our bad luck with the draw continued. Tom replied that it was either that or ask Trevor to pull a few strings with the boss. Trevor would have to use his influence from afar as he was in France and wouldn't be able to make Chelmsford on Tuesday. Mick was unavailable as well, but Patrick planned to make the circuitous train journey from York, and both me and Pete were declared runners. This would be race seven and we were still waiting to get all five of us present to see our filly in action.

27 August 2018

The Gypsy Spirit fairy tale continued. Tom had entered his star two-year-old for a six-furlongs listed race at Ripon. Gypsy Spirit went into the contest with a rating of 92 which was ten pounds below several of the opposition. What a screamer she ran! Tucked in behind horses, she was pulled out wide by Jack Mitchel inside the final furlong, and finished with a flourish, bearing down on Sporting Chance who had a diminishing head to spare at the line. Once again, Tom's filly had completely outrun her odds of 20/1 displaying the qualities of pace, persistence and toughness which are the hallmarks of all good racehorses. I'm sure her owners were absolutely thrilled with their filly's effort, despite the fact that she could be marked down as a slightly unlucky loser. I thought the handicapper would raise her into the high nineties for that effort, more than 30 pounds ahead of Free Love. The curve continued to be upwards for Tom's stable star. Meanwhile, mission control was still waiting for take-off for Free Love.

Free Love and Charlie Bishop in the paddock at Chelmsford.

13 Chelmsford Part II

28 August 2018

Unsurprisingly, Prince Of Rome was all the rage. The early 9/4 had disappeared and it looked like he would end up close to even money. Whether it was stable confidence, or the public latching onto what they thought was a lenient handicap mark, I don't know. It was probably a bit of both. We weren't fancied and once again I had my obligatory fiver each-way at 25/1. We might just sneak into a place, I thought. Not for the first time I reflected that we could finish fifth from that draw and still have run well.

My brother Pete was visiting for a few days and staying with us while he caught up with some old friends. He used to come down from Altrincham quite regularly but, quite understandably, he had been a less frequent visitor during the last two years since mum died. Pete thought a trip to Chelmsford would fit in nicely with his itinerary. It was still schools out for my youngest, Joe. He would be back at sixth-form soon following his impressive GCSE results. He was definitely up for the trip, especially as he had never been to Chelmsford before. The party became five when Trevor sent a message saying that although he couldn't make it, his wife, Fay, was keen to go if I could squeeze her into the car. No problem at all. The more the merrier for the quick jaunt up the A12 to the badlands of Essex.

We left in plenty of time, everybody happy to go along with my growing obsession about getting to the races well before proceedings started. Our race was first up at 4.50pm and we were on the road heading for the Dartford Crossing by 1.45pm. I calculated that we would get there for 3pm, which would leave plenty of time to relax, read the Racing Post and see our filly in the pre-parade ring. We could eat afterwards and digest the merits of Free Love's performance before meandering home, perhaps via one of the many village pubs that Essex can count as its hidden gems.

Wrong, wrong, wrong. Google Maps showed an ominous block of red where Princes Road used to be and advised us to cut across the marshes at Crayford to join the crossing approach nearer to the tunnel entrances. But Google Maps, BBC local news and the AA traffic service were all way off the pace. About two furlongs from the slip road that led to the tunnels, the traffic slowed to a standstill. At first it looked like the type of tedious congestion that afflicts this part of the world even at 2pm on an unremarkable Tuesday, but after twenty minutes, of no movement it dawned on all of us that something was seriously wrong.

The ETA went up and up. At first our phones warned of a fifteen-minute extension to our journey. Then forty, then fifty, then an hour. At 3pm we still hadn't moved and were stuck in a queue on the northbound carriageway. We couldn't even raise the white flag and turn around to head home where we could watch Free Love run on television.

Poor Fay. Poor everyone. I'm not good in these situations. I've been able to control my temper when faced with abusive parents, chair-hurling children, awkward members of staff, unreasonable school governors, and mad Ofsted inspectors. But traffic jams? Everyone and everything was a 'f**king disgrace'. Just in case anybody missed my subtle analysis of events, I repeated the profanities several times in a raised and increasingly exasperated voice. It didn't make me feel any better. All it did was make me think back to my Dad who worked in construction all his life yet never once swore at home. I was falling well short of his impeccable example. Anger, guilt, shame, desperation, remorse. I knew racehorse ownership would feature these emotions but not on a static carriageway straddling the Thames Estuary marshes. It wasn't worse than Kempton though. I had to hang on to that.

The news was contradictory. Jennie sent a text to say both the bridge and the tunnels were closed but emergency services hoped to get at least one tunnel back in action within the hour. Other updates suggested that the closures were 'indefinite'. What did that mean? You'd be better off in Limbo. Two lorries had apparently been involved in a serious crash on the southbound approach to the bridge but as one was overhanging the northbound lanes, it was a safety-first approach, and nothing was moving in either direction.

At about 3.10pm, the traffic started to creep forward. One of the tunnels was open! Progress was infuriatingly slow, and we didn't emerge into Essex until just after 4pm. The ETA was now 5.05pm. That was fifteen minutes to make up. But we were never going the pace to be in contention. I don't know how the traffic could still be so heavy, but it was making it impossible to claw back the time. As we snaked our way through rush-hour Chelmsford, we conceded defeat and decided to pull over to watch the race on one of our mobiles.

Easier said than done. The traffic was solid and at post-time I was trapped in a stop-start line of cars queuing behind temporary lights. I thrust my phone into Pete's hands and asked him to get the race up on the Racing Post app. He was no longer the talking formbook, reading out information about runners and riders. He had been promoted to commentator and race analyst with a specific brief to focus his full attention on Free Love. As we were barely moving, I was able to glance over a few times to catch a glimpse or two of the action. I saw us last into the straight. I saw something bolt clear (Prince Of Rome) and caught an orange jacket working its way into third place, never threatening the leader but finishing well enough.

Third! Last into the straight from our bad draw, but in the prize money.

I don't know what I felt, but it wasn't elation. Our filly appeared to have run a really solid race from another hopeless draw, but my owner's experience being limited to some choppy, streamed images fleetingly viewed on a mobile phone in a crawling Vauxhall Zafira somewhere on a Chelmsford ring road, was not what I had anticipated when I held my pride and joy for an impromptu photo shoot at the Tattersalls sale in October.

We arrived about 15 minutes after the race had been run, and by the time we picked up our passes at reception and made our way into the owners and trainers' bar, Free Love was back in the racecourse stables being readied for her short journey home. Neither Tom nor Jackie were present. Both had gone to the Doncaster yearling sales in search of another Gypsy Spirit. Patrick had made it, so at least we were represented. We'd sent him messages about our plight, which in his brave new smartphone world he had actually picked up.

Patrick seemed happy enough when we finally met up. He had managed to have a word with Jack Mitchell afterwards, who felt that Free Love had handled the track better following her first experience a fortnight ago. He was pleased how she kept on in the straight but felt that when she hit the line our filly had little extra to give, confirming that five furlongs was as far as she wanted for the moment. Maybe so, but I was encouraged by how much better she was now settling compared with the very headstrong behaviour she had shown at Yarmouth and Sandown. I'd yet to see a replay of the race on a decent screen. That would have to wait until I got home, but from what I could tell from the race video available on my phone, we would never have beaten Prince Of Rome, although we might have been a clear second granted a better draw.

Tom called about an hour after the race. He was very upbeat about our filly's performance, especially given her third dreadful draw on the bounce. He had already spoken with Jack, who confirmed what he said to Patrick about the five-furlong trip. This was the only time that neither he nor Jackie had made it to the races and it was good of him to call in person. I agreed that it was another solid run and, more importantly, Free Love seemed to be maturing and had definitely benefitted from her two runs in quick succession at Chelmsford. Tom wished us better luck with the journey home and said that he'd post a quick update over the next few days to let everybody know how our filly came out of the race. When our conversation ended, it occurred to me that the next time I spoke to Tom it would be to tell him that we were moving Free Love to another trainer.

We stayed for something to eat and watched a few races, hoping that the roads would have returned to something like normal by the time we left. Joe drew my attention to a Dutch Art gelding trained by Ed Dunlop who was dropping back in trip and feasibly treated in an ordinary looking mile handicap off a mark of 71. I hadn't had time to look at the race having been consumed with the Free Love feedback and analysis, so decided to go with Joe on this one. Top French jockey Gerald Mosse steered Global Art to a clear-cut success. I had a fiver to win at 6/1 and gave Joe a tenner out of the winnings as a token of my appreciation. That was another triumph to swell parental pride in the boy. A decent set of GCSE results had been backed up by astute analysis of the *Class 5 Bet toteexacta At totesport.com Handicap*, and we were both the richer for it.

There was no respite on the roads. The whole of the Dartford Crossing remained closed and there were reports of drivers and passengers stuck on the southbound bridge approach with no means of escaping, as they were beyond the last motorway exit. We would have to drive through London and cross the Thames via the Blackwall Tunnel.

It took us three hours to get home. The crossing remained closed for 15 hours and the next morning BBC News showed pictures of stranded motorists being put up in the bed department of IKEA in Thurrock. There's always somebody worse off. Miraculously, the two lorry drivers involved in the collision that caused the carnage received only minor injuries. Nobody was seriously hurt and there were no fatalities, which made it all the more perplexing why 'Owner Misses Race' wasn't the screaming headline in the following morning's tabloids. I know, I know. It wasn't a matter of life and death. It was only a horse race.

A collector's item. The QEII bridge finds a quiet moment.

30 August 2018

Two days later, on a sunny but fresh Thursday evening, I visited Sedgefield racecourse for the first time. An educational connection brought me there. I started my teaching career at Oakfield Junior

School in Dartford in 1990 where I first met Colin Turtle who was more or less in the same boat. We had both worked in other fields before deciding to teach, so we already had plenty in common when we turned up for our first day as classroom teachers in the September of that year. After our initial stints at Oakfield, we took different paths. Colin ended up as Head Teacher of High Firs Primary School in Swanley where he is still at the helm today.

Colin isn't a racing fan but enjoys the occasional day out. He's a bit of a lucky mascot as he accompanied me to Nottingham during the 2009 October half-term to see South Cape have his last run of what had been a winnerless season to date. The unlucky sequence ended there with a nice win in decent class 4 handicap, a race the horse would win again the following season. This doesn't lead us immediately to Sedgefield, I admit, but Colin's wife, Emma, is a Geordie girl and every summer the Turtles spend time with Emma's family in the north east.

For a number of years, Colin had tried to persuade me that a short break in Emma's neck of the woods during the school summer holiday would be fun, especially as it could feature a visit to Sedgefield races which has a popular evening fixture towards the end of August. The timing had never been quite right though, either being too close to my annual pilgrimage to York or clashing with the bank holiday weekend which was often a busy time for us at home. On this occasion, however, the schedule looked manageable and we decided to commit to a two-day break which would also take in visiting my elder brother, Paul, who lives in Durham and, like younger brother Pete, has been a less frequent visitor to the south since mum passed away.

That's how we ended up at Sedgefield. Paul has never shown an interest in racing and I was surprised and pleased that he took up my offer to get him a ticket for the meeting. I'm not sure what he made of it, though. Sedgefield is pleasant enough but it's a real country course with sheep grazing on the farmland that borders the track. The facilities are fine but it's not Sandown with its manicured lawns, smart champagne bars and spacious grandstands, and after losing a fiver each-way on the first race Paul closed his wallet and exhibited body language suggesting that he was at a loss to understand the appeal of the experience.

I enjoyed it and it was a fairly interesting meeting. There were three Irish winners on the card, two for Gordon Elliott and one for Gavin Cromwell. The latter's winner was Running In Heels, an appropriate name on an evening when there was no shortage of women vying for the best dressed lady award. I'm not sure how the finances worked for these invaders from across the Irish Sea. All three won just under £4k each and by the time race entry, jockey and travel fees were deducted, I reckon the winning owners saw less than three grand each. That would cover a shade more than one month's training fees, but don't get me started on that again.

Our grand tour of the north east killed several birds with one stone, if I'm still allowed to use that saying. We caught up with my brother Paul, met up with Colin and Emma, ticked Sedgefield off the list, and instead of having to make a separate journey to Mick Appleby's yard in Oakham to discuss Free Love's move, I arranged to make a flying visit on the way home. It would be a very short detour as Mick's yard is about 15 minutes' drive off the A1.

We had all agreed that our filly was on the move, whatever the outcome at Chelmsford. There may have been a change of heart if she had won by five lengths throwing handsprings, but that unlikely event would only have delayed the inevitable. For the long-term future of the partnership, we needed to move away from Newmarket.

14 Last Roll

31 August

We set off for home at around 10am. I arranged with Mick's racing secretary, Jane Hales, to drop in at lunchtime. I knew it was very unlikely that Mick would be about, but at least it would give me a chance to have a quick look around the yard and confirm that there was definitely still a space for Free Love.

We ended up running late. For no obvious reason, the traffic was heavy on the southbound A1 as soon as we got beyond Darlington. Who knows, perhaps it was the early surge of racegoers heading for Wolverhampton. It became a stop-start chug all the way down the A1 and the 1pm rendezvous time, which had looked easy to make, was becoming more like 2pm. I thought I had better stop and phone Jane to let her know about the forced change of plan as racing stables start work early and are generally quiet from lunchtime onwards. I needed to make sure that she knew we were definitely coming.

We made it just before 2pm. Initially I overshot Mick's stables which are located in Langham, about three miles outside Oakham. It's not an area I know well. I'm always driving past it at speed, usually on my way to or from York. For years I'd been promising myself that I would make a brief visit to Oakham to catch up with a former colleague who retired and relocated there. Anne Bickers organised the support for children with special educational needs at Edenbridge Primary School, where I had my first headship. We'd kept in touch by swapping handwritten letters once a year which we both really enjoyed doing. Anne brought me up to date with retired life in rural Rutland and I briefed her on the continuing challenges and rewards of primary school headship as I edged towards retirement. I promised myself that I was going to make a visit one day to see Anne and her husband Robin, but unfortunately it wouldn't be today.

The sign at the entrance of Mick Appleby Racing could be described as small and understated. That was my excuse for flashing by it, driving at speed in an effort to make up time. 'Much haste and little speed,' my dad was fond of saying.

We turned around and made our way through the opening to Mick's yard. It soon opened up quite dramatically to reveal a large complex, housing a mixture of old and new stable blocks to the right, with circular horse exercisers and turn-out pens in front of them. There was a lot of land here. Apparently, it used to be a polo centre and Mick had inherited some of its benefits, including large indoor and outdoor schooling areas.

All was quiet and calm as we made our way to the office, which was easy to find. Jane greeted the three of us with the type of friendly smile that made me feel we'd get on well. She knew the background story from my emails and was aware that this was a quick visit to shake hands on the move. I was just about to give her a recap when Mick appeared. Despite the baseball cap pulled down to protect his eyes from the sun, I recognised him straight away.

I was surprised to see him as I was sure he must have had horses at one of the many meetings taking place that day. Jane had told me that he was very hands-on and was not the type to stay at the yard when he had runners to look after. For that reason, she thought it was unlikely that we would bump into Mick when we made our flying visit. It turned out that he had a plane to catch later on as he was off to Ireland to look after Greatest Journey, who was running in the Irish Cambridgeshire at the Curragh on Saturday. Mick had picked up this Godolphin cast-off for 3,000 guineas in the November sales – quite a reduction on the 240,000 guineas the horse had cost as a yearling. Greatest Journey had already been runner-up in two class 2 handicaps for his new connections and was rated 95. It didn't look like a bad bit of business to me. As we walked round the yard, Mick explained that he liked to buy his horses once, 'They've had a zero or two knocked off their price.' He was a shrewd realist. Maybe it was only romantic dreamers like us who bought yearlings.

We had a lovely fifteen-minute tour of the facilities. Jennie, Joe and I patted a few horses, viewed the impressive outdoor schooling yard which must be the size of a football pitch, and saw the land where Mick intended to build accommodation for stable staff. I told him that I wouldn't want his mortgage, and with a chuckle he agreed. This was quite some commitment from somebody who is clearly not averse to taking risks but does so in a quiet, unflashy way.

As we walked, we chatted about the particular circumstances of Free Love and the North South Syndicate. A bit like how we named our filly, I felt I could do with another digital recording, this one summarising why we were making our move. I'd already talked to one or two people who were interested in the thinking behind the decision and heard myself repeating the same phrases again and again. No problem with the way Tom Clover had treated us…paying for the kudos of having a horse at Newmarket…heath taxes…higher daily rate…too southern-focussed…may need to attract more partners…long-term need to reduce overheads. And so on, and so on.

I was very candid with Mick. Free Love would have to be entered for the sales – the entry deadline was just over a week away – and would only be withdrawn if everyone wanted to continue and could afford to do so. That seemed unlikely if things carried on as they did, which left us with the option of trying to get a few more on board to keep the project alive. Mick's more competitive rates would help with that, but he needed to be aware that he might have our filly for only two months. That meant no more than three runs to turn things around.

The journey home was dreadful, but at least it gave me plenty of time to think about how I would break the news to Tom. I told Mick that I would have done the deed by Monday morning and he would be able to contact Wroughton House later that day to arrange when to collect Free Love, which he anticipated would be at some point next week. Mick knew that we weren't leaving under a cloud. All our training bills had been paid promptly. There had been no rows with Tom, but Mick was a realist and knew that when a trainer loses a horse in such circumstances, a frosty reception may await the new handler.

I suppose I was expecting a frosty reception from Tom. I wasn't naïve. Tom had been good to us right from the start, providing video updates on progress and always happy to spend time with us at the races or during a hastily arranged stable visit. He was going to be disappointed, especially as Free Love had shown that she was capable of winning a little race. After all of his hard work, we were going to move a race-fit filly who was might be on the verge of winning, only he wouldn't get any credit if that happened.

Ideally, I wanted to visit Tom in person to break the news, but that didn't look possible. I couldn't do the next day (Saturday) and a stable visit on a Sunday would be a no-no. This left me with the option of getting to Newmarket early enough on Monday to make sure that I could communicate the bad news before Jane or Mick rang to make the arrangements to collect Free Love. I didn't want that. It would be like a scene from a bad film. I arrive and give the unwelcome news. I depart in silence and five minutes later Tom's phone rings. Camera zooms in on his dejected face. 'Hi Tom. It's Mick. I think you know why I'm calling…' Worse still, I arrive five minutes **after** Mick makes contact. No, I couldn't face any of that. It would have to be done by phone tomorrow.

1 September 2018

The appointment that prevented me from driving to Newmarket was a medical one. During my late thirties, I suffered from severe achilles tendon pain which forced me to pull out of the last month of the football season. I remember it was February 1997 and I was a few weeks off my 40th birthday. I was playing for Old St Mary's first team in a home league game at Hall Place in Bexley, and my right tendon was giving me real problems. I struggled through the match, but we lost 5-0, a defeat which more or less ensured we would be relegated. I decided to try and sort out the tendon over the next few months and resume playing in September, if that was possible.

A combination of physio and a decent rest did the trick, and I returned to football the following season, although I didn't play outfield for the first team ever again. I would have loved to make a first team appearance as a forty-year-old, but I did that a few years later in my new goalkeeping role. I also played outfield again for the twos and threes and thought I had left my tendon problems behind. Six months after retirement everything flared up again and I was even experiencing pain when ambling round Dartford golf course.

I very rarely visit my GP. I always take the view that things will heal over time, perhaps being guilty of over-optimism. It's the same dollop of misplaced optimism that made me think we could buy a Molecomb winner for 10,000 guineas. In football, it made me believe that when we took the pitch we were going to win, regardless of the scale of the task.

One of the most enjoyable seasons I ever had was when me, Pete and another club stalwart, Paul Burton, ran the third team which was made up of the three wise men, their seventeen-year-old sons, and the friends of their sons. We had to wait until our penultimate league game of the season to secure our only win (a scrappy 2-1 victory against the second bottom side) yet in the sixteen games that preceded that epic success, I started every one of them thinking that we were going to win. Being on the wrong end of a 4-0 score line after twenty minutes was usually enough to extinguish such ill-judged confidence. Another golfing pal, the witty and unfailingly polite Clive Ahmed, once told me that optimism was the wrong word for this type of self-belief. He suggested delusional was a better choice. Maybe so, but I think I'll stick with hope. There must always be hope.

After six months of pain, I threw in the towel and visited my GP who referred me for an ultrasound scan at a clinic in Gravesend. The appointment was for 9.30, giving me no chance of getting to Newmarket at a time that would be remotely convenient for Tom. I had already made up my mind that after the scan I would phone Tom. The horses would have finished their early morning work and it would be a good time to catch him, I reasoned.

In my head I rehearsed what I would say to Tom as I sat in the waiting room of the clinic. It's easy to back down in these circumstances. Easy to convince yourself at the last minute that perhaps we should carry on and things would somehow get better. It's easy to think like that because it avoids an unpleasant duty and the upset and confrontation that may accompany it. But it's always best to take a deep breath and see things through, especially if it's not a snap decision but something that's been considered very carefully. In any event, I told the others that I would do it and make all the necessary arrangements. Sounds like a funeral.

I was seen fairly promptly and was back in the car half an hour later. This was it. I would call Tom now. He picked up quite quickly and sounded as if he was outside, probably somewhere around the yard. After exchanging brief pleasantries that confirmed that we were both 'fine', I came straight to the point.

'There's no easy way of saying this Tom, but we're moving Free Love to a different trainer.'

Tom gave a snort of a laugh that summed up his feelings of annoyance and disapproval. I tried to reassure him that this was a purely practical decision and in no way reflected any unhappiness with how he had handled Free Love. Where was that digital recording? I heard myself going through the list of reasons. Heath taxes...too southern focussed...To each point Tom gave a monosyllabic reply. 'Yes. Yes. Yes.' He clearly just wanted to hang up, but I managed to keep him on the line long enough to say that I'd be sending him a detailed email confirming the decision and it would contain a summary of the reasons for the move.

Did I blame Tom for appearing to be irritated and upset? Not really. I expected it, if I'm truthful. Some prospective owners visit you about buying a yearling. You agree to advise them on all aspects of the project. You meet them at the sales and help them to make their purchase. You break in the youngster and send regular video updates about progress. You look after the filly with care, ensuring that she is physically well and happy in her environment. You take her to the verge of being able to win a race, and with two months left to the sales the filly is removed and sent to another trainer. How did I think Tom was going to react? But there were no regrets. It was disappointing for Tom and some might think it was 'bad form' to move our filly, but I knew it was the right thing to do for the future of the North South Syndicate.

That afternoon I went to Sandown. I treated myself to annual membership when I retired and, on some occasions when not going with friends or family, I went solo and had a quiet day at the races. I was happy to strike up conversations with other members or the handful of enthusiasts sitting on the benches dotted around the pre-parade ring. If not in a sociable mood, I would retreat to the members' lounge and read the Racing Post. Today I felt like being alone with my thoughts.

Andrew Lloyd Webber's Too Darn Hot powered home in the Group 3 Solario Stakes. He was clearly a youngster with a big future ahead of him and already there was excitable talk about next year's Classics. Tom had a runner in the last, but I had already decided that I wouldn't be staying for the finale. I think it may have been too soon to look each other in the eye and shake hands.

2 September 2018

I chewed things over during the rest of the weekend and was determined to part with Tom in the most positive way possible. I had promised to send him an email that summed up the reasons behind the decision to move Free Love. In the end, it repeated everything we had discussed as a group, everything I had said to Mick when visiting his stable, and everything I had rehearsed in my head, over and over again before I spoke to Tom:

Dear Tom,

I suppose I should not be surprised that you were disappointed to learn that we were moving Free Love to Mick Appleby's stable, but I do not wish to part on bad terms. We have had a thoroughly enjoyable experience with you and the purpose of this email is to thank you for everything you have done for us.

You and Jackie have been very generous with your time throughout, and on behalf of Mick, Patrick, Peter and Trevor, I must express our sincere gratitude for the personal attention you have given our modest project. Every bit of your input has been much appreciated. Your help at the sales, the regular updates we received right from the beginning, the time you afforded us when making stable visits, and assistance with all aspects of admin, are just some of the things that made our ownership experience with you so positive. I have been fulsome in my praise of the service we have received when chatting with other owners at the races.

Our decision to move Free Love has nothing, therefore, to do with any dissatisfaction with the way you have looked after either her or us. As I tried to explain during our brief telephone conversation, the move is based on practicalities.

I have been very candid with Mick Appleby that the most likely outcome is that Free Love will go to the sales at the end of October unless we can persuade a few more brave souls to join us. Given the partnership's make up, I think we are more likely to do this if we are based more centrally. It is also undeniable that our costs will be reduced as Newmarket is a relatively expensive place to keep a horse in training - although I am well aware that your rates compare very favourably with many others.

Things may have been different if we had an 80 plus handicapper on our hands and the five of us thought that we could carry on as we are. But even then, the travelling for our northern partners would have remained an issue.

I had hoped to be able to inform you of our decision in person but Wednesday or Thursday was the earliest I could get to you and it was agreed by all that if we were going to move, we should do so as quickly as possible given the closeness of the sales. I will be paying the August bill in the morning and understand that a final invoice will follow. Mick Appleby will be in touch with you to discuss collection arrangements.

As I stated at the start of this message, I have no desire to part on anything other than good terms. I will finish by reiterating my thanks for everything you have done for us and wish you and Jackie all the best for the future. I am sure your career will go from strength to strength and I will watch your progress with great interest.

Kind regards, Tony Linnett, On behalf of The North South Syndicate

4 September 2018

Things moved quickly. I had already let Jane know that I had spoken to Tom about our decision. She and Mick wasted no time in sorting things out. By 2pm I received an email telling me that Free Love had arrived safely at the yard. I was quite taken aback by the speed of events. Although Tuesday had been discussed, I thought that would be the very earliest the move would be completed. A little later that afternoon, Jane Hales sent a short update:

Hi Tony,

She is sooooo pretty and so gentle!!

Thanks for confirming your contact details and returning training agreement. I look forward to hearing from you and reporting about Free Love's progress!

Jane

I couldn't help but smile at Jane's observation. Like a parent being told that their child had settled in well during their first day in the reception class, I was beaming with pride. And like most proud parents, the feedback was further evidence of what I already knew. Our little girl was absolutely gorgeous!

The handicapper had been less fulsome in his praise. Rather oddly, he had dropped Free Love two pounds following her gallant third at Chelmsford. Unsurprisingly, the winner had been given a whopping 12 pounds rise to 84, but two or three who finished behind us had only been dropped a pound. On the face of it, the BHA assessor had been kind to us. Perhaps he took the view that this was Free Love's seventh run and that she was fully exposed, with any improvement likely to be minimal or even non-existent. Yes, I was biased, but her last two runs had been from dismal draws which had palpably disadvantaged her. I honestly thought that she could be rated around three pounds better on both occasions. Our new rating of 63 looked slightly insulting to me. We were better than that, surely?

It all happened that day. Free Love moved, the handicapper made his weekly adjustment to official ratings, and Tom got in touch

Hi Tony,

There are no bad feelings at all - I completely understand the logistics of everything and the cost of having a horse trained in Newmarket. I am sure you can understand our mild frustration that she is now handicapped to win and with a couple of suitable races just around the corner, there is a good chance she will go in for someone else, with my team having done all the work - you can see that this would be disappointing, especially in a small yard where every winner counts. It also came as a bit of a shock with the sales just a couple of months away and in all my years I haven't know a horse be moved so close to a sale and towards the end of the season.

I said on the phone that there is no problem and there really isn't.

All the best, Tom

It was a gracious reply. I emailed Tom to tell him that I heard every word he was saying and that I owed him a bottle of champagne. The matter was now closed. It was time to commence what might be the short, final chapter in the Free Love story.

5 September 2018

I thought it would be useful to give Mick Appleby a synopsis of the story so far:

Morning Jane,

I thought I'd provide Mick with some useful factual information and a few thoughts then let him get on with it. Don't worry, we won't be the constantly interfering types!

First of all, Free Love is NOT eligible for auction races. Despite paying Tattersalls their full commission, we are classed as a private sale and my representations to the BHA have fallen on deaf ears. We still qualify for median auction races.

Free Love has a full-brother (Lawless Louis) and a full-sister (Lydia's Place) who both won races and had ORs in the mid-70s. They both trained on were but were restricted to 5 furlongs for virtually their whole careers. Our filly looks like an out and out sprinter as well.

There is no doubt that Free Love was immature and babyish to begin with and, although her work at home had been good, her debut was an absolute nightmare - tailed off and beaten nearly 30 lengths! She now looks much more like a racehorse but still tends to be keen early on. We've never tried just letting her go, but when she over-raced early on at Sandown she didn't get home (decent class 4 handicap admittedly and a very stiff track).

I think she's likely to be better on a flat turf track and her best run was probably at Yarmouth where again she pulled hard early on. Her last two runs have been at Chelmsford where she has run well from poor draws. I think the handicapper must have been feeling a bit sorry for her as she was dropped two pounds for finishing third and would meet the 4th, 5th, 6th and 7th on either the same or better terms. She has plenty of early pace and we reckon that, given the right conditions, she could run to about 70 as she did at Yarmouth, and under top weight on her nursery debut at Lingfield.

Finally, she is slightly offset which made Tom reluctant to try her on an undulating track which means Brighton, Epsom, Goodwood etc were never considered despite the relatively easy nature of the five-furlong tracks there.

That's my view for what it's worth. Not sure if the others would all agree but I think they'd go along with most of it.

As you know, we moved for two main reasons. One was to escape the high training costs of Newmarket which may give us a chance to bring in a couple of more owners to keep the partnership going. The second reason was that our two York based partners, Patrick and Mick, have had a rough deal with the travel and it would be good if we could find a race closer to them for Free Love's stable debut. There is a nursery at Catterick on 22/9 that might suit. Before that there are a couple of opportunities at Beverley on 19/9. If all of those come too soon, there are further opportunities later on at Nottingham and Catterick.

In the end, however, we leave it to Mick to do what he thinks is best for the filly. Hope these observations are a help rather than a hindrance! Regards, Tony

I wasn't really expecting a reply. It was just some information for Mick to digest. I didn't think that there would be a constant stream of information flowing from Langham about Free Love. I couldn't see there being a WhatsApp group for every one of the one-hundred or so horses that Mick had in training and had forewarned the boys that this would be the case. It was inevitable that things would be less personal given the scale of Mick's operation. There was also a difference in styles dictated by personality. Tom came across as outgoing and chatty, while Mick appeared more inclined to keep his own counsel.

I'd done my bit. I'd provided some useful facts and made a pitch for a few races. The nursery handicap at Catterick on 22 September looked particularly interesting. Mick had taken charge of a race-fit filly and Catterick gave him three weeks to assess how well Free Love had settled and if she was ready to race. It was up to him now.

7 September 2018

Jane emailed to confirm that Free Love had been entered in the Tattersalls HIT (horses in training) sale. This would initially cost the syndicate £325. Many horses would be entered for this sale, but quite a few would end up being withdrawn. Perhaps sensing that a sale is imminent, plenty of animals in the HIT catalogue put their best hooves forward in September or October, win a race and are promptly withdrawn. Mind you, this would be at a fair cost to the existing owners. There was a £250 penalty for making a withdrawal after 21 September and further penalties for those making even later decisions. If Free Love showed enough in her final couple of runs to convince us that we could afford to continue with the partnership, but didn't provide the conclusive evidence until a few days before the HIT sale, the total for the entry fee and all penalties would be around £1,000. We'd cross that bridge if and when we came to it.

14 September 2018

It had been a quiet week so, with my interfering owner's hat on, I emailed the racing office to enquire about progress. I asked Jane if Mick was pleased with the way Free Love had settled in and had he given any thought to possible races for her. Jane replied later that day to confirm that Mick was pleased with Free Love and would start to look for suitable races next week. It was nothing very definite. It was close to no real news at all. But when dealing with racehorses, no news is definitely good news. There is so much that can go wrong and for that reason a short message, tentatively suggesting that things were on track, was received with a sigh of relief.

15 September 2018

Kew Gardens ground out a game win in the final classic of the season, the St Leger at Doncaster. It's the oldest of the five classics and perhaps my favourite of them all. I love the speed of the Guineas and have marvelled at the stellar performances of Wollow, Zafonic, El Gran Senor, Dancing Brave and, of course, the breath-taking Frankel. I've admired the combination of pace, balance and stamina of Epsom Derby heroes such as Grundy, Shergar, Sea The Stars and Golden Horn. But the saying goes that the fittest horse wins the 2,000 Guineas, the luckiest horse wins the Derby, and the best horse wins the St Leger.

There's a grain of truth in that glib adage. The first classics come very early in a young three-year-old's career, being run on the first weekend in May. Epsom is a rollercoaster of a track with its steep downhill descent to Tattenham Corner and a home straight camber that can see tired horses wobble and shift left like drunks returning home from a late-night party. It's been the home of many hard-luck stories, best summed up in two words - Dancing Brave. But by the time the St Leger arrives on the flat racing scene in September, these young three-year-old horses have matured and the searching mile and three-quarter test on Town Moor's flat, galloping track offers no hiding places. Stamina, grit and sheer class win the day and past winners like Bustino, Commanche Run, Reference Point and Conduit have proved to be real Titans of the turf. Somewhere deep in Free Love's ancestry, you'll find a St Leger winner. If you look hard enough you can find all sorts of things in a horse's pedigree, including enough evidence to suggest that a five-furlong nursery handicap is within the grasp of a 63-rated great, great, great grand-daughter of an equine star of the past.

By the end of the day, Mick, Patrick, Pete and Trevor had confirmed that they had topped up our racing account to the tune of £500 each. That took our individual investments to £7,300. The total ploughed into the Free Love project was therefore £36,500. We now had enough money in the pot to pay all training fees until the end of October when the adventure would finish, unless our fortunes on the track took a sharp upturn.

It's all relative. For some, throwing another seven or eight grand into the account could be done without too much thought or pain. Others work until they nearly drop and retire with less than that in life savings. Could I afford another year? Yes, I probably could. The mortgage was paid off, and my teacher's pension was better than most and could service the bills – providing they weren't big monthly training fees. However, we hadn't inherited fortunes or bought property to rent out. There were no big investments in stocks, shares and bonds. You know the old saying. We were always too busy working to get rich. We were comfortable enough, though, and being reluctant to invest a significant amount of extra cash in Free Love (or another horse for that matter) was not on the grounds of poverty. We just had other priorities. Matt and Celia were in their twenties, living in rented accommodation in London and might very shortly need a hand with property. Joe would need some help with university if he chose to go. And the family home would require some help too. The twenty-year old kitchen needed gutting and I was resigned to the creation of a downstairs toilet which was part of Jennie's masterplan designed to scupper the creation of my bloodstock empire.

A downstairs toilet. Don't get me started on that one. I had resisted its installation for ages on the grounds that the larder was handy and, in any event, many Edwardian homes (our house was built in 1904) didn't even have an indoor facility, and children slept five or six to a bedroom as well. Or was that the Victorian era? The latter point was originally used to question the wisdom of converting the loft into a fourth bedroom. But Jennie countered with Victorian life expectancy figures resulting from over-crowded, unhygienic lives of grime, and more potential horse ownership money was lumped onto the mortgage instead.

Over the years, whenever a big home improvement project was proposed, I often joked that we could defer it and spend the money on a Galileo yearling instead. This quip got very few laughs and Jennie's usual retort was that it would be, 'Over my dead body.' I teased her saying that this would be a good name for the horse, especially as with seventeen letters and spaces we could register our equine purchase as Over My Dead Body as opposed to the dismal Overmydeadbody. The former could just about win a Classic – certainly be placed in one - the latter would be hard pressed to cut the mustard in a class 6 seller at Brighton.

But can you imagine where Downstairstoilet would end up? Some racecourses put on occasional class 7 races which are pitiful affairs, unless your horse wins one, which Lightning Spirit did for me and several other deliriously happy Heart of the South owners on a cold October evening at Kempton in 2011. Racehorses named Downstairstoilet are made for such low-grade contests. No, we'd just sort out the kitchen, convert the larder into a toilet and resist the temptation to buy another horse. If Free Love didn't work out, I could always go back to penny shareholding with Heart of the South – or maybe organise a racing club myself?

The family pet. Joe, Jennie and Tony make a visit to the stables in July.

15 Catterick Bridge

17 September 2018

The deadline for Catterick entries was fast approaching and, at risk of being branded a nuisance at an early stage with Mick, I decided to send a friendly prompt via email:

Hi Jane,

A couple of the boys were asking if either the Catterick nursery (closes today) or the Lingfield one next week were on the horizon as they would need to make arrangements if they are. Have let them know that the picture may become clearer during the week.

There's also been talk of a flying stable visit later this month, but I can contact you later about that.

Regards, Tony

There had been a few WhatsApp messages flying about regarding a stable visit. I was the only one who had been to Mick's yard and thought it would be a good idea if we could find a date that suited all five us. Perhaps similar to our Huntingdon jaunt, we could have a day at the races at somewhere like Leicester, stay over and go to Langham the following morning. There was enthusiasm for the plan, but it all depended on where Free Love ran next.

I didn't get a direct reply to my email but received an answer of sorts later that afternoon. When the entries for the Catterick nursery handicap were published on the Racing Post website, Free Love appeared in the list of twenty-one possible runners. It looked tough enough for a class 5 handicap for horses rated 0-75. The fairly recent rule change that allowed horses rated 76 and 77 to enter as well, had attracted Raypeafterme (I won't comment on the name) whose

BHA mark was 77. He would be allowed to run providing the race wasn't oversubscribed with horses rated 0-75.

The reason for the competitive looking nature of the race was twofold. First of all, there was no shortage of horses with this rather ordinary level of ability. Secondly, the prize money was better than the majority of similar races could boast. It was £8,600 in total and the winning owners would receive close to £4k once all deductions had been made. There was also prize money down to eighth place. It remained to be seen if Mick decided to make any more entries later in the week but at least we had one target in our sights.

19 September 2017

The WhatsApp group was buzzing. Free Love wasn't entered for Lingfield and everyone agreed that if we ran at Catterick then a trip to Leicester a few days later wasn't on the cards. The stable visit would have to be put on hold. The likelihood of our filly going to Catterick began to look stronger when a provisional jockey booking appeared next to Free Love's name. Scrolling down the entries showed that a number of horses already had a jockey booking which is an indication of the intention to run but not necessarily a solid commitment. Next to Free Love was the name Theo Ladd (5).

Theo who? I follow racing closely, but it tends to be at the top end, and I don't really have a handle on the smaller stables putting out runners in modest races at provincial tracks. I am even less familiar with the many young apprentice jockeys working hard to make a breakthrough in the sport, and I'm ashamed to say that Theo's name was unfamiliar to me.

I could see from the figure in brackets that he was still claiming five pounds which meant Free Love would carry a relatively low weight if she got into the race. If Raypeteafterme ran, he would be lumbered with a topweight of 9st 9lbs, and as we were rated a full 14

194

pounds inferior, Free Love would carry a stone less. Theo would then take off another five pounds because of his apprentice's allowance bringing the burden actually carried by our petite filly down to 8st 4lbs. That looked like a pretty good racing weight to me.

20 September 2018

Final declarations for Catterick were due by 10am. I planned to be around and about, half-heartedly applying preservative to the garden fence so that I could keep an eye on progress. I logged onto the BHA website at about 8.30am and navigated to the Catterick card which showed the current status for all races. On the left was the figure showing how many horses had been entered at the five-day stage. On the right in red text was the number already declared to run. You couldn't tell which horses had been declared, just the number so far. Occasionally a three would become a four or in another race a six become a seven, as more entries were made. It was like watching creosote dry.

By 9.30am, our race was already showing nine runners and I was bracing myself for a double-figure field, a prospect that may have persuaded Mick not to declare Free Love. I went back to the garden for another perfunctory bit of brushwork. When I returned, the deadline had passed and the numbers had been replaced with greyed-out hyphens. The race had closed.

It was about half an hour later before I could access the confirmed runners. Raypeteafterme was at the top of the pile carrying 9 Stone 9 pounds but my eyes had already skipped over the rest of the runners and locked on number nine, Free Love 8st 9lbs to be ridden by Theo Ladd (5). Catterick here we come.

21 September 2018

The Catterick going leading up to the race had been good to firm but late on Thursday a Yorkshire deluge had made a significant impact on conditions and the word 'soft' now appeared in the going description. We didn't need that. The only time Free Love had encountered soft ground was on her second run at Nottingham where she showed up well for a long way before getting tired, prompting Josephine Gordon to say that our filly didn't appear to enjoy the mud. It was only her second run though – her first proper one if you discount the debacle of her Kempton debut – so we didn't know for sure whether or not she could handle soft ground. It was a worry, nevertheless.

I'd given up on the garden fence at this point. I think I'd managed three panels, but the excitement of Free Love's declaration made it difficult to concentrate on the complex task of moving a brush up and down the thirty or so slats that made up each section. I needed to get back to the burning question of the day. Who was Theo Ladd?

I decided to do a bit of research via the Racing Post website. Theo's current strike rate for the season really made me sit up and take notice. It was 14%. That's a phenomenal ratio for a young apprentice, equating to a winner every seven rides. I looked at the current leaders in the 2018 flat jockeys' championship and saw that 10 of the top 25 riders had strike rates that were the same or inferior to Theo's. True, Theo's figures were based on only a dozen or so winners, but it was still impressive stuff. His claim was reduced from seven pounds to five pounds after he rode his twentieth career win in the summer, but that five pounds looked as if it might be great value given his current form.

I watched some of his recent rides via the Racing Post video replays and I liked what I saw. I'm no horseman and I can only go on my experience as a watcher of the sport, but he looked neat, balanced and happy to keep his horses out of trouble by riding them close to the pace. I didn't trawl through the internet or Facebook to find out anything about his background. Maybe he was another young Irishman trying his luck on the other side of the water. I'd soon find out. For now, it was enough to know that young Theodore was a jockey with potential who looked like a good booking for Free Love. Theo would do for me.

Travel plans for tomorrow were coming together. Unfortunately, Trevor had a wedding service to conduct so once again a full-house would elude us. For Patrick and Mick, Catterick was less than an hour's drive heading north on the A1. It was a long haul for the southerners, so Pete and I decided to leave at 8.00am sharp.

The journey from Dartford was a shade under four and a half hours in 'normal' driving conditions. As Free Love's race was due off at 3.35pm, this allowed for plenty of slack. We definitely didn't want to do Catterick on a day return basis, and Patrick kindly offered to find room in his house for both of us on Saturday night, which was much appreciated.

I spent a bit of time looking at the opposition. The eleven-runner race didn't look quite so strong, now that a few of the more likely winners had decided to give it a swerve. I couldn't fancy Raypeteafterme, and it had nothing to do with his name. He'd been pitched into the valuable sales race at York following a promising win in a class 5 novice event at Thirsk, but he'd finished 19th of 20 at York beaten 45 lengths. You couldn't put him on the shortlist whatever the excuse was for that well below par effort. Of the others, Richard Fahey's Essenza took the eye but she was still a maiden. So were we, for that matter. Tom Dascombe's March For Men looked to have a handy weight but nothing jumped off the card and many of the runners were bought cheaply and trained in the north. There was no lightly-raced, Newmarket-trained, Godolphin-owned 100,000 guineas yearling lurking towards the top of the handicap who had the ability to bolt-up before going on to achieve much greater things.

Catterick is nearer to Edinburgh than Newmarket, which obviously deters many big (and small) southern trainers from sending their horses there. Had Free Love still been with Tom, it was very unlikely that we'd be heading for North Yorkshire tomorrow. We'd have all agreed that six or seven hours each-way in a horsebox was too much for a young filly, never mind the huge transport costs involved.

I didn't spend hours perusing the form. I thought we'd have plenty of time to analyse the opposition while on the road tomorrow. I checked the betting and saw that 8/1 was the best price on offer for Free Love. I didn't think she was going to get much shorter and decided to wait until the morning before having a bet.

The last task before bed was a weather update. By late evening the going at Catterick had been changed to 'good to soft.' Another dry but cool day was forecast, and hopes were rising that by the time Free Love cantered down to the start, the ground could actually be good. A final bedside check of the Met Office app confirmed this likelihood, and I drifted off into deep, dreamless sleep despite my excitement about the next part of the Free Love story which was about to unfold in North Yorkshire.

22 September 2018

I was shaved, showered, dressed and downstairs by 7.15am. It's easy to spring out of bed for these things. A mug of tea was steaming next to the keyboard as I checked the news. No rain. That was a positive, as was the forecast which stuck with the prediction of a cool but dry and overcast day at Catterick. The going description remained good to soft but the turf would be drying all the time. Free Love was now best priced at 12/1 with Paddy Power. As I'm a penny gambler who doesn't bet regularly with a range of bookmakers in my ruthless search for value, I had to retrieve my login details in order to deposit £25 into the account, which seconds later I placed on Free Love to win. If Jennie was awake, she'd be urging me to go each-way and she'd be right. I could always have a fiver each-way 'saver' on course, I thought.

The next task was to send a quick message to Ronan. I first met Ronan at either Cheltenham or Royal Ascot about 35 years ago, I can't remember which. He lived in Bristol where he was friends with Pete's younger brother, Roly. I think that's how we met but can't be sure. What I do remember is that all the girls liked Ronan. With his lilting Northern Irish accent, mop of unkempt black hair, dark eyes, cherubic lips and youthful face, he was surely a descendant of one of the great romantic poets. His penchant for drinking and gambling added a frisson of destructive charm.

Ronan is a genuine horseracing aficionado. He knows his stuff and I greatly enjoyed his company at the races. I made a point of seeing him whenever we visited Bristol, whether it was for a football tour with the fledgling Old St Mary's FC, or a party. On one occasion I remember being with him in the infamous *Dug Out* club (a cramped cellar bar accessed by a narrow single-staircase, which surely made it a strong candidate for best west Country fire-trap) until 2am following a day at the Cheltenham Festival. I was somehow in work seven hours later and although I wasn't teaching at the time, thank God, it wasn't an experience that I rushed to repeat.

After starting our family, wild trips to Bristol became a thing of the past and I lost touch with Ronan. I hadn't seen him for 25 years until a visit to Newbury for the 2015 Greenham meeting. I went with Pete, and as the course had arranged to host a beer festival, we took the train. It was a beautiful day towards the end of April. Summer was definitely on the way and the card was full of young horses in the spring of their careers. Halfway through the meeting, Pete said to me that he thought he had seen Ronan. I asked him if he was sure, to which Pete replied that he was as sure as he could be.

'Did you approach him?' I enquired

'I didn't really want to in case it wasn't Ronan,' was Pete's odd, but rather in character, reply.

Well we did approach him, and it really was the same Ronan Maguire of Royal Ascot, Cheltenham and Bristol fame. What a great chance encounter. We had a beer in the sunshine, took photos, swapped details and proceeded to back Intilaaq who hosed up by eight lengths in the mile maiden race. I've kept in touch ever since with 99% of the content of all communication being about horses.

I made sure Ronan was in the picture with the Free Love saga and provided him with a little analysis in advance of each race. Some were quite detailed but this morning's one was brief:

Hi Ronan,

A very quick update before I head for the frozen north! Can't see how Mick Appleby will get our filly to improve in less than three weeks but then he doesn't have to. The form of our last two runs from rubbish draws at Chelmsford stands up well and the handicapper was very kind to us after our last effort. Just wish the rain had stayed away, that's the only real negative.

The jockey is an apprentice really going places and we have to fancy our chances with another five pounds off her back. Wouldn't put you off a few quid each-way. Just the going to be a bit concerned about but it's drying all the time.

Regards, Tony

The email was sent at 7.32am and less than half an hour later I had picked up Pete and we were heading for the Dartford crossing. The roads looked clear but we both knew that could change. We had a Racing Post and plenty of time to assess Free Love's opposition in forensic detail. The last journey, as far as this story was concerned, was about to begin.

We were both in good spirits, although we realised that this was a seminal event. It was hard to see what the next move would be if we couldn't go close off a mark of 63 in the *Class 5 Book Now For Saturday 20th October Nursery Handicap*. The story was getting towards the final chapter perhaps, but a win could change everything. Not only would it be a welcome injection of cash into the racing account, it could be a stepping stone to maintaining the partnership. The significance of the day wasn't lost on either of us.

Pete was the talking formbook. We decided to go through each runner in alphabetical order, objectively weighing-up their chances and considering the level of threat they represented. First on the list was Amazing Alba, a Helmet filly trained by Michael Dodds in County Durham. This filly had been placed on her first two starts before finishing fifth in her fourth and final run which was in a class 5 novice race at Ripon. Surely that wasn't as good as our Yarmouth third or our most recent effort behind Prince Of Rome? Next was Big Ace, a 15,000 guineas Kuroshio colt trained in Yorkshire by Tim Easterby, son of Sea Pigeon's trainer, Peter Easterby. Big Ace had won one of his nine races, but his form had a regressive look about it. In his most recent run, he was last of four beaten over 12 lengths in a Beverley handicap. We put a line through that one.

And so it went on. Nearly all the runners were bought cheaply, had only shown bits of promise in the handful of races that made up their lifetime form, and were trained north of the River Trent. I suppose Free Love fitted in well, but I couldn't get away from thinking that the official rating of 63 underestimated our filly. Yet despite our exhaustive analysis of the opposition and the logic behind the thinking that Free Love was well handicapped, the further we sped up the A1 the more my confidence waned. They say a little knowledge is a dangerous thing. Maybe so, but it can certainly confuse.

We didn't even know what to make of the draw. It was a first visit to Catterick for both of us and the five-furlong course could be described as quirky. I looked at recordings of previous sprint races at the track which showed horses going slightly downhill for the first furlong, before encountering a steeper descent which swept them towards a left-hand kink at the three-furlong marker. It was then a sharp uphill stretch before the course levelled out for the final two furlongs. If anything, it was downhill again close home. We were drawn nine and it was hard to tell whether that was good or bad. Logic seemed to suggest that a low draw towards the inside had an advantage but other 'experts' provided data to say that middle to high was the place to be. It was anybody's guess.

We were making great time. The Dartford Crossing was empty. The M25 and M11 motorways were on their very best behaviour and we were soon speeding up an uncannily quiet A1. I have an obsession about not stopping until over halfway on any journey, both in terms of miles and time, and for that reason we took a break at a small service station somewhere between Newark and Doncaster. I can't remember exactly where, but it was under two hours from Catterick.

About half an hour before taking our break, Pete told me that Free Love was out to 16/1 with one firm of bookmakers. I raised an eyebrow at that. It was far too big a price and I was sure it wouldn't last. On her public form, there was no way Free Love was a 16/1 shot. I thought I could have my fiver each-way saver at that price when we stopped.

Half an hour can be a long time in horseracing. When we entered the functional service station café, with its drab orange and yellow colour scheme, a quick check of my phone revealed that Free Love was now as low as 13/2 in places! A text message from a golfing pal asked if we fancied Free Love in the light of the price collapse. I replied saying that we hadn't spoken to the trainer about it but on her public form alone you had to fancy our filly off a mark of 63. I concluded by saying that despite the concerns about the ground, we'd be disappointed if we weren't in the shake-up.

It's a strange old game, full of conspiracy theorists. Mick Appleby is renowned for taking on horses and getting them to improve. Sometimes his winners have been very well backed which has meant that punters keep a watchful eye on horses making their debuts for the Appleby yard, tracking any moves in the betting market that may indicate stable confidence. Could Free Love be an Appleby coup? Many punters want to believe that the whole game is about inside information, secretive gambles, smoke and mirrors. A market move may suggest that people 'in the know' are putting their cash down. This in turn prompts others to jump on the bandwagon and join the gamble.

Of course, some of these gambles are backed up by sound inside information. A young horse making its debut may have impressed on the gallops encouraging owners (and stable staff) to place some hefty bets on the creature. A horse slipping down the handicap following a few runs on unsuitable going and perhaps over unsuitable trips, finds an opportunity over its optimum distance and on ideal going. Connections back him, confident that he can show his true colours off a lenient handicap mark. Some win, some lose. There was nothing mysterious about Free Love's market move. Our small bets wouldn't have budged the early morning price. Maybe a couple of Mick's stable hands felt that their new inmate had settled in nicely and was working well. Perhaps they felt that she worked better than a 63 rated filly. Maybe they hadn't, but once the 16/1 became too tempting for some punters and the price was clipped to 14/1, then 12/1, plenty others would have followed thinking they had latched onto a Mick Appleby gamble.

I'm not sure what level of improvement everyone expected Mick to find in the 18 days Free Love had been in his care. True, it was a change of scenery and routine for our filly, and although I had no doubt that Mick had a knack of improving horses, it was a bit much expecting him to work his magic so quickly. Rather ironically, the Racing Post inaccurately reported that it was only five days since Free Love moved stables. What punters thought the Langham magician could do in that short time, I really don't know.

Mick received a fit horse from Tom and probably did nothing with her for the first week, allowing her to settle into her new surroundings. After that, I guess it would have been a few pieces of fast work before being sent to Catterick. But I don't know because I didn't ask.

The betting confirmed the open looking nature of the race with Essenza heading the market at 4/1. There was absolutely no way that Free Love was a 16/1 shot. That's why she was backed.

We were owed a charmed run on the roads and we got one. We were bearing down on Catterick Bridge racecourse before 1pm. As we entered the car park, I realised I hadn't received a reply to my email asking who would be looking after Free Love. Mick had two runners at Catterick, but I presumed he would be supervising his horses at the big meeting at Ayr. I parked up and checked my phone. I had a missed call from a number I didn't recognise. I returned the call and was greeted by a husky Barnsley accent. It was Mick. He said that he's picked up my email on his phone and apologised for not being able to make it, but he was in Sweden looking after Big Country who was due to run in a listed race at Bro Park on Sunday. Kirsten was the lady who had driven the horsebox and she would be in charge. All was good. I thanked Mick for calling and wished him luck with Big Country but didn't bother to ask him how he thought Free Love would go and he didn't volunteer any information either. This was clearly a very English coup.

It was grey and cold when we clambered stiffly out of the car. If you looked hard enough, it was just possible to see the location of the sun hidden behind layers of thick Yorkshire cloud. We were about 300 yards away from the owners and trainers' entrance, when a smiling lady on a golf buggy whizzed over to offer us a lift. We declined the kind offer feeling that we needed to stretch our legs.

The course was surprisingly busy even though it was nearly an hour before the first race. We walked past a reasonably sized grandstand on our right and, once at its end, climbed up a few steps to get a look at the five-furlong course. It was an odd one, with the stalls set up high and the descent to the left-hand kink at the bottom of the hill clearly visible. I wasn't sure whether it would suit Free Love, but it looked a fast track and I knew from previous race times that this must be the case. The course record was a fraction over 57 seconds and sprint race times often broke a minute providing the going wasn't too testing.

The owners and trainers' bar was a relatively small, one-level building situated directly opposite the parade ring. It was no more than twenty paces from the door of the bar to the rail of the paddock. Everything about the course had a compact feel making the healthy crowd already there seem even bigger. There was no sign yet of Patrick or Mick who had abandoned the train and were coming together by car, so Pete and I decided to wait for them in the bar where hot food was provided for owners.

It wasn't Sandown, but it was very friendly, and I was in no mood to be critical of the beef bourguignon which bore a close resemblance to the rather bland casserole that my dear old mum used to inflict upon us from time to time. We finished our lunch and almost

205

immediately afterwards Patrick and Mick appeared. We were soon in deep conversation about our chances and the significance of the race for the future of the North South Syndicate.

Patrick noted that the official going description had been changed to 'good'. That update had passed me by, and I was pleased to receive the news. We agreed that it would be interesting to see what the ground looked like during and after the first race which was a six-furlong novice contest for two-year-olds.

The six-furlong course was on the main track, so it meant turning sharply left soon after the stalls opened. A low draw looked a real bonus and so it proved to be. Hollie Doyle pinged the start on Fognini and stayed glued to the rails as she made the 180 degree turn into the straight. She never looked like getting caught and pushed out her willing partner to a gritty half-length success.

I walked down to the finishing line to inspect the turf. It hadn't looked great during the race. Large divots were being kicked up in the straight and hard though runner-up, Napahook, had tried to reel in Fognini, his progress looked a little laboured in what appeared to be quite testing ground.

It didn't look good. The ground staff were already out with their forks and spades trying to repair a chewed-up home straight, especially close to the fair rail where all of the field had galloped. The race time was announced, and it was nearly five seconds slower than the standard time for the six-furlong trip. No way was that ground good. The word 'soft' had to feature somewhere in the going description. 'Good' was a bad call.

Hollie Doyle repeated the trick in race two, making all on Two Blondes, who overcame a wide draw to surge home over two lengths clear of her toiling rivals. It looked a faster pace to the eye, but the race time was still moderate enough, edging towards four seconds slower than the standard for seven furlongs. The ground was good

206

to soft at best, I thought. Again, nothing looked remotely likely to catch Two Blondes as she powered home towards the far rail.

As I waked back to the bar, I saw that Kirsten must have found her man. Either that or Pete had got lucky. He was standing just outside the building chatting away with an unfamiliar lady. I wondered how they had found each other so easily, and got my answer when Kirsten revealed that Jane had told her to look out for a tall man. Pete was an uncompromising third team centre-half who stands at around six-one or six-two and as I am an inch or so taller, Kirsten had a pretty good chance of tracking down the North South Syndicate.

Kirsten was in charge of operations at Catterick. Mick often has runners scattered all over the country and I imagine he needs a fair bit of help getting horses to different courses, sometimes using people who may not be permanent members of staff. This was the case with Kirsten, who worked with horses and was licenced to drive the horsebox. She told me that she and her husband helped to break-in young horses for Mick, and also gave a hand on race days if Mick was stretched. She had two young stable girls with her to assist with the preparations for Free Love and Mick's other runner, Sellingallthetime (no comment), who ran in the class 4 mile and three-quarters handicap which preceded our race.

We all decided to pay a bit of extra attention to this contest, as Theo Ladd was booked for Sellingallthetime. It wasn't a bad little race and the progressive Trouble And Strife, trained by Sir Mark Prescott, was a well-backed favourite. Our Mick pointed out that it was the sole ride at Catterick that day for Luke Morris, so we all had a small wager at around 3/1. There was neither trouble nor strife for Sir Mark's young stayer who powered clear inside the final furlong. Theo kept Sellingallthetime handily placed just behind the leaders, but he could never mount a serious challenge, although he did keep on well to be third, only four lengths behind the decisive winner. That wouldn't have done young Theo's confidence any harm, I thought, given that this was his first ride following a break from racing of more than a week.

This was it. The time had come to head to the pre-parade ring, which I took to be the small loop attached to the main paddock. There wasn't a horse in sight when we arrived, but Kirsten was there, deep in conversation on her mobile phone. Apparently, there had been a mix-up which she hadn't been able to resolve and had enlisted the help of Mick in Sweden. Kirsten's licence allowed her to drive the horsebox, but it didn't permit her to enter the stables where she was needed to saddle the Appleby runners.

Mick had been on the phone from Sweden trying to persuade racecourse officials that Kirsten should be allowed into the stable block, as the two young girls travelling with the horses couldn't be expected to take full responsibility for this important task, but his urgings fell on deaf ears. His solution was to get hold of another trainer who had runners at Catterick to ask if they could help out, just keeping an eye on things to make sure everything was in order. By the time we got to Kirsten she was reporting back to Mick that everything had gone well with his first runner and the matter was in hand.

What made matters worse was the fact that Kirsten couldn't even get near enough to peer into the stables, as they are located on the other side of a busy public road that runs right through the town. At the back of the paddock, work was in progress on stabling boxes and it may be that, at some point in the future, the detached buildings across the road will no longer be needed. I'm not sure if that's the plan, but for now traffic has to be stopped at regular intervals to allow racehorses to walk to and from the main racecourse; a charming throwback to an earlier age.

Kirsten assured us that everything had worked out well for Sellingallthetime, and Free Love would be brought over very shortly to join us. The first one to appear was a smallish chestnut. Clearly not us. Next was a strapping bay colt, with similar colourings to Free Love but considerably bigger and without the tiny bits of white just above both rear feet. Then an attractive bay filly walked in, sporting a noseband and a plaited mane. I almost needed a second look. It was Free Love, but I'd not seen her in a noseband before and the plaited mane was new as well. She looked so pretty! It was like seeing somebody at a formal evening do who rarely dresses up and you barely recognise them at first. I'm not saying that Free Love wasn't turned out well by Tom, but the new look certainly took the eye.

Who's a pretty girl? Free Love looking good in the Catterick paddock.

Free Love went straight into the main paddock and we followed her in. Theo wouldn't be with us for a bit yet, but he would be easy to find in his garish orange and green silks. After a few minutes of nervy chat about the draw and the going, and who we thought the main dangers were, our jockey appeared. I was expecting a diminutive Irishman and was taken aback when Theo offered a firm handshake to all present while maintaining confident eye-contact and introducing himself in an accent that was more educated home counties than west coast of Ireland. Maybe my next horse should be named Dontjudgeabookbyitscover.

We were on the same wavelength about the going. Theo confirmed it had plenty of give in it but felt that our wide draw could be an advantage as he could stick to the fresher ground in the middle of the course when the field fanned out into the straight. He was articulate, socially confident and personable. I liked him already.

The word compact could be used again to describe the Catterick paddock. It seemed crowded enough with twelve horses walking around it, and a large gathering of owners and connections looking on from the centre. When the bell was sounded for the jockeys to mount, one of the colts quite near to Free Love started playing up but our filly took it all in her stride, giving the impression she hadn't even noticed her competitor's immature antics. You've done a lot of growing up young lady, I thought to myself as she left the paddock and cantered down to the start, looking relaxed and on good terms with herself.

As we walked to the grandstand, we passed the bookmakers on our right. I saw 10/1 on one board, but it quickly disappeared and soon 8/1 was the best price I could see. I gave up on the idea of my each-way saver. In any event, I didn't need to buy any more excitement. I had a tangible sensation of trembling. It wasn't in the Ealing Comedy sense of being unable to hold a pint of beer without violently shaking and spilling it all over the stooge, but it felt real, the kind of physical agitation associated with worrying about unknown outcomes, especially the ones that are completely out of your control.

At least I managed to hold my binoculars still enough to see that Free Love had arrived at the start and was standing very calmly in front of the starting stalls. Calmer than me, I mused. She was about the fifth or sixth to be loaded and I could see Theo stroking her neck as they both waited for the others to join them. We positioned ourselves for a good view of the race, but not so far up in the stand that it would be difficult to get down quickly afterwards. The runners would approach from our left and we stood about ten steps up, with the winning post no more than twenty yards to our right.

There was no anxious wait on this occasion as the remaining runners were slickly loaded. Valentino Sunrise was last in and when her handler emerged from under the front of the stalls and scampered to the side, the flag fell, and they were off.

Free Love seemed moderately away and slightly squeezed for room in her first few strides. She was far enough back for my liking, with only a couple behind her, one of them the well-supported Essenza who made the type of start that loses sprint races before they even begin. Theo didn't panic and let our filly find her feet. As they ran down the hill, the partnership was towards the outside, travelling sweetly and no more than four lengths off the lead. Jill Rose and Amazing Alba were setting a brisk pace at the head of affairs as the field swept past the left-hand kink at the three-furlong marker. Our filly was visibly improving, Theo keeping her widest of all. The runners met the rising ground a furlong and a half from home, and Theo began to make his challenge. With his stick in his left hand, he gave Free Love a couple of flicks and she responded with a determined looking run up the centre of the track. Raypeteafterme and March For Men's efforts both fizzled out and with nothing else

211

making progress from the rear, Free Love looked the only danger to the two pacesetters.

That split-second when you realise your horse has a real chance of winning is a rare and magical moment. At the furlong pole, it looked as if Amazing Alba on the far side, Jill Rose in the middle, and Free Love nearest the stands were three abreast, but they were still about 200 yards away from where we were standing and our oblique, slightly head-on view made it difficult to know exactly what was happening. That all changed in less than five seconds. Amazing Alba was the first to crack. Her stride shortened as she fell away quickly leaving Free Love with only Jill Rose to overcome. Theo switched his stick into his right hand and following another two flicks, Free Love surged closer to her game opponent as they raced past the half-furlong marker. It was happening. It was really happening.

If the split-second that you know you're in with a chance is magical, the precise moment that you know your horse is going to win is pure ecstasy. Free Love edged slightly to her left and towards Jill Rose in the last fifty yards, but our smart young jockey put his stick down and straightened his charge up with hands and heels as the racecourse commentator's voice rose to a crescendo with the words, 'Half a furlong to go. Jill Rose being joined now by Free Love who's storming home towards the line. Free Love staying on best of all. Free Love beats Jill Rose!'

I can't remember exactly what words I used as Free Love entered those pulsating final 100 yards, but I know I was bellowing. I think I was screaming, 'Come on Baby! Come on Baby!' or something like that, followed by a throaty roar of 'Yeeeessssssss!' as our filly crossed the line. The next moment I was rushing down the grandstand steps with Pete, Patrick and Mick, all smiles, all a bit bewildered, still coming to terms with the reality of our gorgeous little filly finally getting it all together to win a little race for us. I didn't think capturing a class 5 nursery handicap at Catterick could feel so fabulous.

We needn't have rushed. Unlike Sandown, where the winners' enclosure is way beyond the back of the grandstand and can take a few minutes to reach on a busy day, we made it to the enclosure set aside for the first three home in about 30 seconds. Catterick Bridge 1 Sandown Park 0. The runners started to trickle back from the course into the parade ring, those outside the first three staying put for post mortems of varying degrees of grimness. Free Love was one of the last back and it seemed ages before we finally saw a beaming Theo Ladd and his victorious partner stroll into the winners' enclosure to be reunited with the impossibly proud members of the North South Syndicate.

I have no coherent recollection of the chronology of events during that half hour or so immediately after the race. The memories are jumbled, jigsaw puzzle pieces that I know how to put together but always end up doing so in a different order. I remember that it was getting a little brighter and I have photographs of us with patches of blue sky appearing above our beaming smiles. Theo was a happy boy as well. He told us we'd wait a long time before we got one as genuine as Free Love and he talked about getting six furlongs next season – maybe even seven!

Our brave little filly was being walked round, steam rising from her sweating back and neck. We were patting and stroking her, taking turns at capturing pictures on our phones. I suddenly remembered that we should give the two young stable girls a little drink each and interrupted the celebrations to ask the boys to donate a tenner each to the cause. The official photographer was on the scene. Next we were posing for formal pictures, Theo holding Free Love with me and Patrick on the left, Pete and Mick on the right. I was buzzing. I didn't want it to end because the longer it went on the more real it felt, and the more certain I was that our little dream had been realised.

'Horses away,' was the call and with a final pat, Free Love was on her way back to the stables to get ready for her journey home. I hadn't paid too much attention to the details in the back of the racecard, but buried in the small print was a line about the racecourse presenting a memento to the winning owners. The photographer soon had us in a neat group standing behind a small podium carrying the Catterick Races Est 1783 logo on its front. The racecourse announcer congratulated the owners of Free Love as two ceramic mugs displaying the same racecourse logo were handed over in presentation boxes. One or two onlookers may have clapped out of politeness, but it really didn't matter.

A member of the racecourse staff had been hovering in the background while all this was going on. She was there to make sure that everything went smoothly and to invite us for a glass of champagne in the private box overlooking the winning post, which is reserved for such occasions. The room was comfortable and neatly presented. We were handed a celebratory drop of bubbly and asked if we would like to view the race again. We didn't need a second invitation.

It was at this point that I thought I should check my phone. I'm not a great social media user and with a small number of racing pals who have kept in touch with the Free Love story, I wasn't expecting an avalanche of congratulatory messages. I had missed calls from Joe and Mick Appleby. A text message from Jennie read, 'Hope you are in the champagne bar having wrung out your hankie. Well done Free Love!' I phoned Joe first. I can't remember what I said, but he knew how much this meant to me, so not many words were needed. I called Mick who sent his warmest congratulations. He said he hoped that we had backed her, because he hadn't! Maybe it was just as well that I didn't seek out his thoughts on our chances in advance.

I watched the replay of the race in between these conversations. I noticed that Trevor had responded to some pictures that had been put up on the WhatsApp group and gave him a quick call as well. The wedding had finished in time for him to watch the race and his voice was full of the euphoria felt by the rest of us. I also spoke to Kieran at some point, but that may have been a little later. Mick Corrigan mentioned in passing that Tom had come across well in his interview on ITV Racing ahead of Gypsy Spirit getting stuck in the mud in the *Group 3 Firth of Clyde Stakes* at Ayr. But it wasn't a day for comparisons. It was all about Free Love. I could let go of Gypsy Spirit now.

It was fascinating seeing the race again on a big screen. Two things stood out. First of all, Free Love settled beautifully. Maybe the sluggish start did us a favour. There was none of the headstrong behaviour that we saw at Yarmouth and Sandown. I thought again how much those two Chelmsford experiences had taught her. Secondly, she was well on top at the finish and won going away. There may have been a length between the first five or six horses with two furlongs to run, but at the line it was more than two lengths back to the third with the fourth a length further away. The time was relatively quick as well, outside the standard by a fraction over two seconds. On easy ground, our filly had failed to break 60 seconds by a whisker.

There was the inevitable talk about how the handicapper would view the race. It looked a competitive heat run in a comparatively quick time, which accounted for the fact that the field didn't finish in a heap, something that often happens in these sprints. It looked to me that we could expect a five or six-pound hike in the weights when the adjustments were published on Tuesday. That would bring Free

215

Love's official BHA rating up to 68 or 69. It also put us on an upward curve and would surely encourage us to do everything we could to keep the partnership going.

Our filly would probably have one more run, perhaps two, before her date with Tattersalls on 1 November and she'd have to perform pretty badly to force us to sell up and dissolve the partnership. Even if some of us wanted out, and some wanted in, with a win next to Free Love's name I was already thinking about the possibility of keeping things goings by getting some new partners to buy into the North South Syndicate. If that was needed to keep the dream alive, I was fairly confident I could now make it work. Buying into a 69 rated winner with the potential to win again was a much more attractive proposition than taking a share in a 63 rated maiden. Best of all would be the five of us agreeing to carry on as we were.

We headed back to the owners and trainers' bar to sort out plans for the evening. Patrick already had a commitment. He was going for a fancy meal with Sally, a gourmet experience that he and a number of his York friends had signed up for long before Catterick was on the horizon. But like all good epicureans he felt that the quality of the gastronomic experience would greatly benefit from a couple of pints of fine ale in a local pub after the dessert course and its accompanying glass of Sauternes had been polished off. He had somehow persuaded Sally that this would be a good way to conclude their sophisticated night out.

Patrick needed to head off to get ready but the rest of us stayed to catch another race or two before making our move. Mick was in no hurry and happy to travel back to York with me and Pete.

When your luck's in. The last race we watched was a very ordinary seven-furlong class 6 handicap. Our Mick's betting market analysis revealed that Redrosezorro had been backed at fancy prices in the morning. He hadn't been successful since winning the same race a year ago off a mark of 62. Twelve months later, his rating had slipped back to the same level and with almost identical conditions today, it was easy to see why his connections thought that he could bounce back to form. The icing on the cake was the jockey booking. Theo took the ride. I had a fiver at 9/2 and watched the price shrink even further to 7/2 at the off.

I think Theo must have been told to keep things simple – get to the front and keep improving your position. He wasn't drawn well in stall eight, but he got a flying start on Redrosezorro which allowed him to gradually edge over to the rail. The partnership led at a decent pace as the field, already well strung-out, hurtled round the tight left-hand bend into the straight. Theo was two lengths up and his mount responded to his urgings to draw further clear, crossing the line with over four lengths to spare with the course commentator talking about Redrosezorro powering home under a positive ride from Theo Ladd. I went back to the winners' enclosure to see them come in. The jockey was beaming as I called out to him, 'It's an easy game Theo!' He nodded at me before dismounting for a chat with another group of delighted owners.

We strolled back to the car. The lady in the golf buggy had clocked off, but we didn't need her services. We were walking on air. The sun continued to burn through the ever-thinning clouds. It was turning into a lovely evening as we made our unhurried way towards York on the A1. As I drove away, I could see in my mind's eye how the evening would unfold. A meal and a couple of drinks in Brigante's would be followed by a pint or two elsewhere. The atmosphere would be serene, infused with a feeling of satisfaction, completion. It was not the end of the story, but if felt like a conclusion of sorts. We would relive the race again and again. We would talk of the past and plan for the future. There was so much to discuss, so much to start dreaming about again.

I turned off the A1 and joined the A59 for York. Pete was sat in the front lost in his own thoughts, Mick was quiet and content in the back. Nobody had spoken for a while.

'Do you know what the best thing about today was?' I asked, interrupting the silence.

'What was that?' enquired Mick in his matter of fact way.

'It happened. It really happened.'

There was no need for further words as the car eased its way through the Yorkshire countryside under the gaze of the low autumn sun and its soft, pallid light.

Storming home! Free Love surges into the lead close home at Catterick.